2006 EDITION

EXPORT PROGRAMS GUIDE

A BUSINESS GUIDE TO FEDERAL EXPORT ASSISTANCE

This guide is the U.S. government's most comprehensive and widely distributed export resource, a listing of all federal government programs that aid U.S. companies in exporting their goods and services around the world. Nineteen different agencies have united to offer this publication and the many programs to help American firms succeed in the global marketplace. Dedicated to improving federal trade promotion programs, these agencies comprise the Trade Promotion Coordinating Committee (TPCC).

For example, Asia Now and Access Eastern Mediterranean are two initiatives that provide exporters with a single point of access for information on regional trade events, business counseling and marketing services, and market research specific to their respective regions. Other regionally focused resources include the China Business Information Center and the Middle East Business Information Center. These centers make available comprehensive Web sites and both offer access to a call center staffed by trade specialists.

For additional information on the listings in this guide or for any export questions you have, please contact the Trade Information Center (TIC), of the U.S. Department of Commerce. The TIC is the first stop for information on federal export assistance programs plus general, regional, and country counseling. The TIC has a team of international trade specialists available to give you tailored export assistance.

To contact a trade specialist, call 800-USA-TRAD(E), e-mail *tic@ita.doc.gov,* or search TIC's on-line resources at *www.export.gov/tic*, where the guide is also available in PDF format.

The Trade Promotion Coordinating Committee

Chaired by the Secretary of Commerce

Member Agencies

U.S. Department of Commerce
Export–Import Bank of the United States
Overseas Private Investment Corporation
U.S. Trade and Development Agency
U.S. Small Business Administration
U.S. Department of Agriculture
U.S. Department of State
U.S. Department of the Treasury
Office of the United States Trade Representative
U.S. Agency for International Development
U.S. Environmental Protection Agency
U.S. Department of Defense
U.S. Department of Energy
U.S. Department of the Interior
U.S. Department of Labor
U.S. Department of Transportation
Office of Management and Budget
National Security Council/National Economic Council
Council of Economic Advisers

Welcome to the 2006 edition of the Export Programs Guide. This guide is the U.S. Government's most comprehensive collection of export-related information. Exporters can consider this book a one-stop shop for listings and descriptions of Federal Government programs that aid U.S. companies in exporting goods and services to customers around the world. The agencies administering these programs are all members of the inter-agency Trade Promotion Coordinating Committee, which I am proud to chair.

Access to information about exporting is more important than ever before, as our national economy becomes increasingly globally oriented. Ninety-five percent of the world's customers now live outside of the United States. For American companies to grow, they need to look beyond our borders.

Exporters are a source of strength for their communities, and for the economy at large. Twenty-five percent of the U.S. economy is trade-related, and roughly one in five manufacturing jobs are export-related. Those jobs offer higher wages than their non-export counterparts.

We applaud your interest in exporting and creating new opportunities for American workers. Please use this guide to learn more about programs that support and promote exports and trade development. By working together, we can keep the American economy strong and dynamic for years to come.

Carlos M. Gutierrez
Secretary of Commerce

This edition of Export Programs Guide was compiled under the auspices of the Trade Information Center. Editorial and production assistance was provided by the International Trade Administration's Office of Public Affairs. Design and composition were done by the Creative Services division of the U.S. Government Printing Office.

Copies of this publication are available from the Trade Information Center, tel. (800) USA-TRAD(E) (800-872-8723) or through the Government Printing Office, tel. (866) 512-1800 *http://bookstore.gpo.gov/*

ISBN 978-0-16-075020-5

Superintendent of Documents stock no. 003-009-00734-8

December 2005

Table of Contents

CHAPTER 1

GENERAL EXPORT COUNSELING AND ASSISTANCE

International Trade Administration, U.S. Department of Commerce

The International Trade Administration (ITA) is dedicated to opening markets for U.S. products and services and providing assistance and information to exporters. ITA units include (1) trade specialists in 108 domestic Export Assistance Centers and 150 overseas offices, (2) industry experts and market and economic analysts, (3) market access experts, and (4) import policy and trade compliance analysts who enforce trade laws and agreements that provide remedies to domestic industries injured by unfair import competition. These ITA units perform analyses, promote products, and offer services for the U.S. exporting community, including export promotion, counseling, and information programs listed elsewhere in this booklet.

Contact: For more information about ITA, call 800-USA-TRAD(E) (800-872-8723), or visit *www.ita.doc.gov.*

U.S. Commercial Service, ITA, U.S. Department of Commerce

The U.S. Commercial Service (CS), a program of the U.S. Department of Commerce's International Trade Administration, helps U.S. companies, particularly small and medium-sized businesses, increase their international market share and sales. Through its global network of more than 1,700 trade specialists located in 108 domestic offices and 150 posts in 80 countries, the CS works one-on-one with companies through every step of the exporting process—helping them leverage world-class market research, promote their products and services in target markets, meet qualified international buyers and distributors, and overcome challenges and barriers they may encounter while doing business in international markets.

Contact: For more information about the CS and its programs, visit *www.export.gov*, or—to speak with a CS trade specialist—call 800-USA-TRAD(E) (800-872-8723).

Trade Information Center, CS, ITA, U.S. Department of Commerce

The Trade Information Center (TIC), a U.S. Commercial Service resource, is the first stop for companies seeking export assistance from the federal government. CS trade specialists working in the TIC

- Advise U.S. firms on all government export programs
- Guide businesses through the export process
- Provide country and regional business counseling on standards and trade regulations, distribution channels, opportunities and best prospects for U.S. companies, tariffs and border taxes, customs procedures, and common commercial difficulties
- Direct businesses to market research and trade leads
- Assist businesses with the North American Free Trade Agreement Certificate of Origin and with other free trade agreements
- Provide information on overseas and domestic trade events and activities
- Refer businesses to state and local trade organizations that provide additional assistance

Contact: For more information, visit *www.export.gov.* To contact a CS trade specialist, call 800-USA-TRAD(E) (800-872-8723), fax (202) 482-4473, or e-mail *tic@ita.doc.gov.*

U.S. Export Assistance Center Network, CS, ITA, U.S. Department of Commerce

The U.S. Department of Commerce, the U.S. Small Business Administration (SBA), the Export–Import Bank (Ex–Im Bank), the U.S. Agency for International Development (USAID), and the U.S. Department of Agriculture (USDA) have formed a nationwide network of U.S. Export Assistance Centers (USEACs). USEACs are located in more than 100 cities throughout the United States and serve as one-stop shops that provide small and medium-sized businesses with hands-on export marketing and trade finance support. USEACs work closely with federal, state, local, public, and private organizations to provide unparalleled export assistance to American businesses trying to compete in the global marketplace.

USEAC trade specialists provide global business solutions by (1) identifying the best markets for their clients' products; (2) developing effective market-entry strategies based on information generated from commercial offices; (3) facilitating the implementation of these strategies by advising clients on distribution channels, key factors to consider in pricing, and relevant trade shows and missions; and (4) providing assistance in obtaining trade finance available through federal government programs, as well as access to state, local, public, and private-sector entities.

Many USEAC offices are co-located with other federal, state, local, public, and private-sector entities—making it easy for U.S. companies to find the help they need.

Contact: For the address and phone number of the USEAC nearest you, see Appendix A, call 800-USA-TRAD(E) (800-872-8723), or visit *www.export.gov.*

Global Diversity Initiative, CS, ITA, U.S. Department of Commerce

The Global Diversity Initiative (GDI), a program of the U.S. Commercial Service, provides services to increase the export of goods and services from women and minority business owners. Specifically, GDI works to engage, educate, and advocate for U.S. women- and minority-owned businesses so that they can tap into growing export markets for their goods and services. GDI also supports the Rural Export Initiative, which provides companies in rural areas better access to export assistance and global market research.

Contact: For more information, call (202) 482-4792, e-mail *global_diversity@ita.doc.gov*, or visit *www.buyUSA.gov/globaldiversity*.

District Export Councils, CS, ITA, U.S. Department of Commerce

District Export Councils (DECs) are organizations of leaders from local business communities whose knowledge of international business provides a source of professional advice for local firms. Closely affiliated with USEACs, the 58 DECs nationwide combine the energies of more than 1,500 volunteers to supply expertise to small and medium-sized businesses in their local communities that are interested in exporting. For example, DECs organize seminars that make trade finance understandable and accessible to small exporters, host international buyer delegations, design export resource guides, and create export assistance partnerships to strengthen the support given to local businesses.

Contact: For more information on DECs, call 800-USA-TRAD(E) (800-872-8723), or visit *www.export.gov*.

Office of International Trade, Small Business Administration

The Office of International Trade (OIT) works with other federal agencies and public and private-sector organizations to encourage small businesses to expand their export activities, as well as to assist small businesses seeking to export. OIT directs and coordinates SBA export finance and export development assistance. OIT outreach efforts include regional initiatives with Brazil, Chile, China, Egypt, Mexico, and Nigeria, whereby SBA's alliances with government agencies for small business in other countries can facilitate trade opportunities in those countries. In addition, OIT develops "how-to" and market-specific publications for exporters.

In assisting small business exporters, OIT oversees SBA loan guarantee programs, including the Export Working Capital Program, which is available through USEACs and SBA field offices across the country. Also through the USEAC network, OIT spearheads the Export Trade Assistance Partnership (E-TAP). The E-TAP program focuses on small groups of export-ready companies, providing them assistance in developing export markets, acquiring orders or contracts, gaining access to export financing, and preparing for trade missions or overseas shows.

Contact: To learn more about OIT, call (202) 205-6720, fax (202) 205-7272, or visit *www.sba.gov/oit*.

SBA
U.S. Small Business Administration

Small Business Development Centers, Small Business Administration

Located throughout the United States, Small Business Development Centers (SBDCs) provide a range of technical and export assistance, particularly to small companies that are new to exporting. Such assistance includes counseling, training, and managerial support. Their counseling services are free to the small business exporter, but there may be small fees for export training seminars and other SBDC-sponsored export events. Many SBDCs are involved in the E-TAP program.

Contact: For more information on SBDCs, call Jorge F. Cardona, Office of Small Business Development Centers, at (202) 205-7303, fax (202) 205-7727, or visit *www.sba.gov/sbdc*. For the location of the SBDC nearest you, call 800-USA-TRAD(E).

Export Legal Assistance Network, Small Business Administration

With a presence in 70 U.S. cities and with the participation of more than 250 attorneys, the Export Legal Assistance Network (ELAN) program is a nationwide group of attorneys in private practice who have particular expertise in international trade and who provide free initial consultations to businesses that are new to export on export-related matters. Issues relating to export licensing, domestic and foreign taxation, tariffs, and intellectual property rights are just some of the topics covered. The ELAN service is available through SBA district offices, the Service Corps of Retired Executives (SCORE), and Small Business Development Centers. For maximum benefit from the session, we recommend that exporters call ELAN after designing their strategic plan so they arrive with specific questions.

Contact: For the address and phone number of the SBA office nearest you, visit *www.sba.gov/oit*, or call 800-U-ASK-SBA. To contact ELAN, call Judd Kessler, ELAN national coordinator, at (202) 778-3080, fax (202) 778-3063, or e-mail *jkessler@porterwright.com*. For a full list of ELAN coordinators across the United States, visit *www.fita.org/elan*.

Service Corps of Retired Executives, Small Business Administration

SCORE, which consists of locally chartered volunteer organizations funded by SBA, provides free, expert, problem-solving assistance to small businesses. Helping American small businesses to prosper has been SCORE's goal since the program began in 1964. SCORE tries to match counselor experience with client needs and provide one-on-one counseling. SCORE also conducts well-developed, pre-business workshops and a variety of business-oriented seminars and training sessions.

Contact: Visit SCORE's home page at *www.score.org*, call (800) 634-0245, or fax (202) 205-7636. To contact W. Kenneth Yancey Jr., SCORE's chief executive officer, call (202) 205-6762.

Minority Business Development Agency, U.S. Department of Commerce

The Minority Business Development Agency (MBDA) is the only federal agency created to specifically foster the establishment and growth of minority-owned businesses in America. The agency's mission is to actively promote the growth and competitiveness of large, medium, and small minority business enterprises (MBEs). MBDA operates the Minority Business Development Center (MBDC) Program and the Native American Business Development Center (NABDC) Program. These programs provide direct business consulting services to minority entrepreneurs. The centers provide the following services: access to markets; access to capital, management, and technical assistance; and education and training. To accomplish this goal, the centers provide entrepreneurial assessments and general business consulting; marketing assistance; loan packaging and other financial consulting; identification of and assistance in obtaining procurement opportunities; education and training; and various other entrepreneurial consulting services. MBDA currently operates 26 MBDCs and 8 NABDCs throughout the United States. MBDA works closely with the International Trade Administration on innovative ways to engage U.S. minority firms in the international business arena. Seminars inform minority firms of the tremendous opportunities available through international trade. MBDA supports several minority trade missions and matchmaker programs and notifies the minority community about all Department of Commerce trade missions.

Contact: To learn more about MBDA, contact Donald Powers at (202) 482-7982, fax (202) 482-3473, e-mail *dpowers@mbda.gov*, or visit *www.mbda.gov*.

CHAPTER 2

INDUSTRY-SPECIFIC COUNSELING AND ASSISTANCE

Manufacturing and Services Industry Officers, ITA, U.S. Department of Commerce

Manufacturing and Services (MAS) is the industry-focused arm of the International Trade Administration. Its mission is to deliver industry analysis and trade policy support to promote the interests of U.S. exporters, especially small and medium-sized enterprises; to forge public–private partnerships to enhance the international competitiveness of U.S. industries; and to initiate industry-specific trade events. MAS industry and international trade specialists work directly with U.S. firms and industry associations to identify overseas trade opportunities and obstacles by product or service, industry sector, and market. MAS analysts also participate in trade policy development and negotiations and advocate on behalf of U.S. companies to help them win foreign contracts. MAS staff members also develop export marketing programs and obtain industry advice on trade matters. They organize executive trade missions, trade fairs, product literature centers, reverse trade missions, marketing seminars, and business counseling. Experts are organized in the following sectors:

- Aerospace
- Automotive
- Consumer goods
- E-commerce
- Energy
- Environmental technologies
- Information technologies
- Machinery
- Metals, materials, and chemicals
- Microelectronics, medical equipment, and instrumentation
- Services and finance
- Telecommunications technologies
- Transportation and machinery
- Travel and tourism

Contact: Trade statistics are available by industry on the home page of Manufacturing and Services' Office of Trade and Industry Information, at *http://ita.doc.gov/td/industry/otea/*. For MAS industry and international trade officers, call 800-USA-TRAD(E) (800-872-8723). To access industry office Web sites, choose “Manufacturing and Services” on the ITA home page at *www.ita.doc.gov.*

Export Advantage Web site for Textiles and Apparel Import Administration, ITA, U.S. Department of Commerce

The Export Advantage Web Site, which is at *http://otexa.ita.doc.gov/ExportAdvantage/ExportAdvantage.htm,* provides information on foreign rules and requirements affecting U.S. textile and apparel exports overseas, such as tariffs and taxes, labeling requirements, and other issues. The Web site also provides information on trade events sponsored by the Office of Textiles and Apparel (OTEXA), as well as directories of overseas buyers and U.S. suppliers.

Contact: For information about OTEXA, visit *www.otexa.ita.doc.gov.* For information on international trade shows and events, call (202) 482-5153, or e-mail *market_expansion@ita.doc.gov.* For assistance with exporting or information on foreign regulations affecting U.S. textile and apparel exports, call (202) 482-3588, or e-mail *exportadvantage@ita.doc.gov.*

U.S. Travel and Tourism Statistical System, ITA, U.S. Department of Commerce

The Office of Travel and Tourism Industries functions as the U.S. federal tourism office. Among its core responsibilities is the collection, analysis, and dissemination of international travel and tourism statistics for the U.S. Travel and Tourism Statistical System, as well as the promotion of international travel to the United States. Information disseminated covers

- Basic market analysis
- Survey of international air travelers (in-flight survey)
- Visitor arrivals (I-94 form)
- U.S. international air traveler statistics (I-92 form)
- Forecast of international arrivals to the United States
- International travel receipts (exports) and payments (imports) data
- Canadian arrivals and visitation program
- Travel Trade Barometer Program
- Travel and tourism satellite accounts
- U.S. Promotion Campaign

Contact: Contact the Office of Travel and Tourism Industries at (202) 482-0140, or visit the home page at *www.tinet.ita.doc.gov.*

EcoLinks, the Eurasian–American Partnership for Environmentally Sustainable Economies, Institute for International Education, U.S. Agency for International Development

EcoLinks is a USAID-funded trade and investment program that supports environmental technology representatives in selected U.S. Commercial Service offices in Eastern Europe and Eurasia. These EcoLinks "tech reps" make use of several tools available from USAID, the Commercial Service, and host governments to identify business opportunities in the environmental sector, link U.S. environmental technology firms with partners in the region, and assist in financing the associated environmental projects.

Contact: To learn more about EcoLinks, call Gerald Gold, Partnership Grants Program, at (202) 712-0263; Jeffrey Orrey, Trade and Investment Program, at (202) 712-1608; or view the home page at *www.ecolinks.org*.

Trade and Technical Assistance, U.S. Department of Transportation

The Department of Transportation's Office of International Transportation and Trade (X-20) serves as the department's overseer on collaborative trade-related initiatives and technical assistance programs. The X-20 office works closely with agencies such as the U.S. Trade and Development Agency and the U.S. Department of Commerce to organize business workshops designed to help establish relationships and share information between U.S. businesses and foreign officials who are likely to make—or to heavily influence—awards of international contracts. Under mechanisms such as bilateral and multilateral agreements, the Department of Transportation's operating administrations participate in cooperative programs and technology initiatives with partners worldwide and promote policies that enhance U.S. industry access to foreign markets.

Contact: The following people can offer assistance: Bernestine Allen, Office of the Secretary of Transportation, (202) 366-4398; fax (202) 366-7417; e-mail *bernestine.allen@dot.gov*; Greg Hall, Maritime Administration, (202) 366-2765; fax (202) 366-3746; e-mail *greg.hall@dot.gov*; Kay Drucker, Bureau of Transportation Statistics, (202) 366-4437; fax (202) 493-0568; e-mail *kay.drucker@dot.gov*; Henry Nevares, Federal Highway Administration, (202) 366-0111; fax (202) 366-9626; e-mail *henry.nevares@fhwa.dot.gov*; Barbara Pelletier, Federal Railroad Administration, (202) 493-6395; fax (202) 493-6401; e-mail *Barbara.Pelletier@fra.dot.gov*; Rita Daguillard, Federal Transit Administration, (202) 366-0955; fax 202-366-3765; e-mail *rita.daguillard@fta.dot.gov*; Rochelle Claypoole, Federal Aviation Administration, (202) 267-8208; fax (202) 267-5047; e-mail *Rochelle.claypoole@faa.gov*; Julie Abraham, National Highway Traffic Safety Administration, (202) 366-0846; fax (202) 493-2290; e-mail *Julie.Abraham@nhtsa.dot.gov*; or Thomas Marchesault, Research and Innovative Technology Administration, (202) 366-4434; fax (202) 366-7431; e-mail *Thomas.Marchesault@dot.gov*.

Office of Fossil Energy, International Programs, U.S. Department of Energy

The Office of Fossil Energy enhances the competitiveness of U.S. industry by supporting domestic fossil energy (coal, oil, and gas) project developers and exporters trying to expand the international sales of fossil energy technology, resources, and services.

Contact: To learn more, contact the following: Judd Swift, deputy director for international affairs, (202) 586-6660; fax (202) 586-4729; e-mail *judd.swift@hq.doe.gov*; home page *www.fe.doe.gov*; Barbara McKee, director, Coal and Power Export and Import, (301) 903-3820; fax (301) 903-1591; e-mail *barbara.mckee@hq.doe.gov.*

CHAPTER 3

COUNTRY-SPECIFIC COUNSELING AND ASSISTANCE

U.S. Commercial Service, ITA, U.S. Department of Commerce

The U.S. Commercial Service helps U.S. companies, particularly small and medium-sized businesses, increase their international market share and sales. Through its global network of more than 1,700 trade specialists located in 108 domestic offices and 150 posts in 80 countries, CS works one-on-one with companies through every step of the exporting process, helping them leverage world-class market research, promote their products and services in target markets, meet qualified international buyers and distributors, and overcome challenges and barriers they may encounter while doing business in international markets.

Much of the trade-related information and many of the trade-related tools the CS offers are accessible through the Internet at *www.export.gov*. Companies can also call 800-USA-TRAD(E) to speak with a CS trade specialist about their specific issues. For hands-on, customized assistance, companies can work directly with CS trade specialists located in any of the CS offices around the country (often referred to as *U.S. Export Assistance Centers*). All domestic CS trade specialists are directly linked to their international counterparts (often referred to as *foreign service commercial officers*) in markets around the world, ensuring that CS customers get the comprehensive in-country assistance they require.

International companies interested in sourcing U.S. products and services can find the tools and information they need on the Web Site of the U.S. Commercial Service post—usually a U.S. embassy or consulate—in their respective country. Alternatively, they can contact the CS post in that country directly. A complete listing of domestic and international locations and contacts is available at *www.export.gov*.

Contact: For more information on the U.S. Commercial Service, visit *www.export.gov*. To contact a CS trade specialist, call 800-USA-TRAD(E) (800-872-8723), fax (202) 482-4473, or e-mail *tic@ita.doc.gov*.

Trade Information Center, CS, ITA, U.S. Department of Commerce

CS trade specialists working in the TIC provide export counseling and assistance on Asia, Western Europe, Latin America, Africa, the Near East, the Western Hemisphere, and the North American Free Trade Agreement (NAFTA). Country-specific counseling is available at no cost on country conditions; commercial laws, regulations, and practices; standards; government procurement; certification requirements; distribution channels; business travel; opportunities and best prospects for U.S. companies; tariffs, taxes, and customs procedures; commercial difficulties encountered in doing business abroad; and other market information. The TIC is the U.S. government's designated point of contact for help with documentation to qualify for NAFTA benefits and other free trade agreements. The TIC, through *www.export.gov*, provides extensive country and regional information, including a downloadable NAFTA Certificate of Origin, a tariff and Harmonized System number lookup tool, and contact information on foreign customs offices and trade offices in the United States.

Contact: For general information on exporting, visit *www.export.gov*. To contact a trade specialist working in the TIC, call 800-USA-TRAD(E) (800-872-8723), fax (202) 482-4473, or e-mail *tic@ita.doc.gov*.

China Business Information Center, CS, ITA, U.S. Department of Commerce

The China Business Information Center (BIC) is a comprehensive resource provided by the U.S. Commercial Service for small businesses that are interested in or are already doing business in China. The China BIC consists of an extensive Web site, a call center staffed by trade specialists, and a China seminar series, which is available nationwide. These seminars provide comprehensive guidance on entering the Chinese market and accurately portray the realities and challenges inherent in doing business there.

Contact: For information on doing business in China, visit *www.export.gov/china*. To contact a U.S. Commercial Service trade specialist working in the China BIC, call 800-USA-TRAD(E) (800-872-8723), fax (202) 482-4473, or e-mail *chinabic@mail.doc.gov*.

Middle East Business Information Center, CS, ITA, U.S. Department of Commerce

The Middle East Business Information Center is a comprehensive resource provided by the U.S. Commercial Service for small businesses that are interested in or are already doing business in the Middle East and North Africa. The Middle East BIC consists of an extensive Web site and a call center staffed by trade specialists.

Contact: For information on doing business in the Middle East and North Africa, visit *www.export.gov/middleeast*. To contact a U.S. Commercial Service trade specialist for this region, call 800-USA-TRAD(E) (800-872-8723), fax (202) 482-4473, or e-mail *tic@ita.doc.gov*.

BISNIS

Business Information Service for the Newly Independent States, CS, ITA, U.S. Foreign Commercial Service, U.S. Department of Commerce

The Business Information Service for the Newly Independent States (BISNIS), an initiative of the U.S. Commercial Service, provides market information, practical advice, trade and partner lead opportunities, and referrals to U.S. and Eurasian companies to facilitate U.S. exports and other forms of business development with Russia and other countries of the former Soviet Union. BISNIS services, which are free for U.S. and Eurasian companies, include

- BISNIS Online (*www.bisnis.doc.gov*), containing the latest market information, leads, and resources for doing business with Eurasia
- E-mail updates on market reports and leads from Eurasia
- U.S. export and partner leads for Eurasia (*BISNIS Trades & Tenders* and *BISNIS Search for Partners*)
- BISNIS FinanceLink, for U.S. companies and companies in the newly independent states that have agreed on a U.S. export transaction and seek financing
- ExpoLink Eurasia, a unique Russian-language promotion tool for U.S. companies' goods and services
- Consultation and guidance for both practical and strategic business development decisions
- *BISNIS Bulletin*, the bimonthly BISNIS newsletter highlighting commercial developments in Eurasia

Contact: For information on doing business in the newly independent states, visit *www.bisnis.doc.gov*. To contact a CS trade specialist working in BISNIS, call 800-USA-TRAD(E) or (202) 482-4655, fax (202) 482-2293, e-mail *bisnis@ita.doc.gov*, or visit *www.bisnis.doc.gov*.

U.S. Embassies and Consulates, U.S. Department of State

U.S. Department of State staff advance U.S. foreign economic policy interests abroad and report extensively on the impact of economic developments on U.S. foreign trade and investment policy objectives. Foreign service officers (FSOs) provide political and economic briefings and advise U.S. firms on the business culture and practices of the host country. They advocate on behalf of U.S. business with key ministries in foreign countries and seek to build foreign government support for U.S. foreign economic policy goals. FSOs are responsible for commercial work in 95 embassies and 35 consulates not covered by the Commercial Service. FSOs work closely with their CS colleagues worldwide.

Contact: For more information, call the U.S. Department of State main line at (202) 647-4000. Visit the U.S. Department of State's Office of International Information Programs at *http://usinfo.state.gov*. Find out more about U.S. embassies at *http://usaembassy.state.gov*.

Regional Bureaus, U.S. Department of State

Country desk officers in regional bureaus in Washington, D.C., maintain regular contact with overseas diplomatic missions and can provide U.S. exporters and investors with economic and political information from both a country and regional perspective.

Contact: Visit the regional bureau's home page at *www.states.gov/countries/*, or contact a particular regional bureau as follows: Africa, (202) 647-3502; East Asia and Pacific, (202) 647-3487; Europe, (202) 647-4174; Near East and North Africa, (202) 776-8457; South Asia, (202) 736-4255; or Western Hemisphere, (202) 647-3341.

Foreign Agricultural Service, U.S. Department of Agriculture

The Foreign Agricultural Service (FAS) maintains more than 60 offices overseas, mostly located in U.S. embassies, to represent the interests of U.S. agriculture and carry out market promotion. The FAS also offers assistance to exporters of U.S. farm and forest products in 20 agricultural trade offices overseas. The FAS supports U.S. food exporters with marketing and assists them at foreign trade shows. Agricultural FSOs perform advocacy activities in policy negotiations, monitor and report on market access, and represent individual U.S. exporters in foreign customs disputes.

Contact: Call FAS Outreach and Exporter Assistance at (202) 720-7420. Call the AgExport Services Division at (202) 720-7420. The FAS home page is *www.fas.usda.gov*.

CHAPTER 4

TRADE CONTACT AND MARKET RESEARCH PROGRAMS

CUSTOMIZED PROGRAMS

International Partner Search, CS, ITA, U.S. Department of Commerce

The International Partner Search (IPS), a service of the U.S. Commercial Service, helps U.S. companies find qualified international buyers, partners, or agents without traveling overseas. CS trade specialists will deliver detailed company information on up to five prescreened international companies that have expressed an interest in the U.S. firm's products and services. Fees depend on the scope of work.

Contact: For more information on IPS, contact the CS trade specialist at your local U.S. Export Assistance Center. For the address and phone number of the USEAC nearest you, see Appendix A.

Gold Key Service, CS, ITA, U.S. Department of Commerce

The Gold Key Service, a program of the U.S. Commercial Service, helps U.S. companies secure one-on-one appointments with prescreened potential agents, distributors, sales representatives, association and government contacts, licensing or joint venture partners, and other strategic business partners in their targeted export markets. Fees depend on the scope of work.

Contact: For more information on the Gold Key Service, contact the CS trade specialist at your local U.S. Export Assistance Center. For the address and phone number of the USEAC nearest you, see Appendix A.

Platinum Key Service, CS, ITA, U.S. Department of Commerce

Through the Platinum Key Service, a program of the U.S. Commercial Service, U.S. businesses can attain comprehensive, customized support on a range of issues on which they need longer-term, sustained assistance. The service is solution oriented and tailored to the client's needs through a mutually agreed upon scope of work. Assistance may include, but is not limited to, identifying markets, launching products, developing major project opportunities and providing government tender support, helping to reduce market access barriers, and providing assistance on regulatory or technical standards matters. Ongoing service is available for six months, one year, or a specified time frame based on the mutually agreed upon scope of work.

Contact: For more information on the Platinum Key Service, contact the CS trade specialist at your local U.S. Export Assistance Center. For the address and phone number of the USEAC nearest you, see Appendix A.

Market Research, CS, ITA, U.S. Department of Commerce

Market Research reports generated by the U.S. Commercial Service cover current conditions in specific country markets and identify upcoming opportunities for generating sales. These reports are produced overseas by in-country experts and are available at no cost to U.S. companies.

Contact: For more information on CS Market Research, contact the CS trade specialist at your local U.S. Export Assistance Center. For the address and phone number of the USEAC nearest you, see Appendix A.

Customized Market Research, CS, ITA, U.S. Department of Commerce

Customized Market Research (CMR) generated by the U.S. Commercial Service produces individual responses to questions and issues related to a client's specific product or service. The research can address issues such as overall marketability of the product, key competitors, prices of comparable products, customary distribution and promotion practices, trade barriers, and potential business partners. Fees depend on the scope of work.

Contact: For more information on CMR, contact the CS trade specialist at your local U.S. Export Assistance Center. For the address and phone number of the USEAC nearest you, see Appendix A.

International Company Profile, CS, ITA, U.S. Department of Commerce

The International Company Profile (ICP) program of the U.S. Commercial Service checks the reputation, reliability, and financial status of a prospective trading partner. A U.S. exporter can obtain this information and detailed answers to specific questions about the prospective partner in a confidential report. Fees depend on the scope of work.

Contact: For more information on the ICP program, contact the CS trade specialist at your local U.S. Export Assistance Center. For the address and phone number of the USEAC nearest you, see Appendix A.

Videoconferencing Programs, CS, ITA, U.S. Department of Commerce

These cost-effective video services offered by the U.S. Commercial Service help U.S. companies assess overseas markets or overseas business contacts before venturing abroad. Companies can use these programs to interview international contacts, get a briefing from overseas industry specialists on prospects and opportunities, or develop a custom solution to their international business needs.

- **Virtual Trade Mission.** This service provides meetings with prescreened international firms via videoconferencing without the cost of traveling overseas. The Virtual Trade Mission focuses on your specific industry and allows you to meet potential partners and get answers to your market questions in an interactive videoconference.
- **Video Gold Key.** This service helps firms identify and meet with prescreened international firms. It includes three to five scheduled meetings with potential business partners and an industry briefing with seasoned trade professionals. All meetings take place through videoconference. Prices vary according to location.
- **Video Market Briefing.** This service provides time-sensitive market research for specific products and services. Benefits include a market-entry evaluation and written report, followed by a videoconference with an industry professional so a firm can get immediate answers to market questions. Prices vary according to location.

Contact: For more information on video programs, contact the CS trade specialist at your local U.S. Export Assistance Center. For the address and phone number of the USEAC nearest you, see Appendix A.

Commercial News USA, CS, ITA, U.S. Department of Commerce

Commercial News USA, the premier export promotion magazine of the U.S. government, is published bimonthly by the U.S. Commercial Service through its private-sector partner ThinkGlobal International. The magazine of U.S. goods and services is distributed (free of charge) to 80,000 prescreened potential buyers and partners in 145 countries.

Contact: For information on advertising in *Commercial News USA*, call 800-USA-TRAD(E), (800-872-8723), or contact ThinkGlobal International at (800) 581-8533. You can visit the magazine's Web site at *www.export.gov/cnusa*.

ELECTRONIC MATCHMAKING AND TRADE CONTACTS PROGRAMS

The Export Yellow Pages®, ITA, U.S. Department of Commerce

The Export Yellow Pages is used by foreign buyers as a reference tool to find U.S. goods and services. This service enables U.S. firms to present their products to a worldwide audience at no cost. U.S. firms can register their business profiles for free at *www.myexports.com.* Export intermediaries such as freight forwarders, sales agents, and other service firms that facilitate export business can also register their business profiles free at *www.myexports.com* in the U.S. Trade Assistance Directory, which is available online and as a supplement within the printed version of *The Export Yellow Pages*.

This program is a public–private partnership between the U.S. Department of Commerce's Manufacturing and Services Unit and Global Publishers LLC of Milwaukee, Wisconsin.

Contact: To register your business profile, visit *www.myexports.com* or call (877) 390-2629. To receive a free copy of *The Export Yellow Pages®* and information on other export programs, contact your local USEAC. For the USEAC closest to you, see Appendix A.

Trade Leads, CS, ITA, U.S. Department of Commerce

Trade Leads, a service of the U.S. Commercial Service, provides U.S. companies with current sales leads from international firms and foreign governments seeking to buy or represent U.S. products and services.

Contact: Trade Leads is accessible at *www.export.gov*.

Global Trade & Technology Network

The Global Trade & Technology Network (GTN) was established in 1994 as a U.S. Agency for International Development trade facilitation program. The focus of the GTN is to facilitate trade between U.S and foreign companies and to develop international markets that bolster steady economic growth both in the United States and abroad. The current Web-based trade platform was launched in 2002 with funds provided by USAID and has since facilitated more than $345 million in potential transactions, generated over 4,000 trade and investment leads, and produced more than 350,000 buyer–seller matches for the 13,000 companies registered on the GTN database. GTN is no longer funded by USAID and is presently managed by International Business Linkages LLC. Through joint ventures, direct sales or purchases, agent-distributorships, and licensing, registered companies are able to establish international trade links and recognize the true benefits of e-commerce. These benefits are available to firms in all industry sectors in the United States and abroad.

Contact: Registration in the GTN program is free of charge, and full details may be obtained on the GTN Web site at *www.usgtn.net* or at the following contact phone numbers: (814) 456-1005 or (908) 668-1865.

Environmental Technology Network for Asia and the Americas, U.S. Agency for International Development (USAID)

The Environmental Technology Network for Asia and the Americas (ETNA) is a U.S. government-sponsored program that collects environmental trade leads from the Asia–Pacific region and disseminates them to U.S. environmental technology and services firms. Established in 1993, ETNA is an initiative of the United States–Asia Environmental Partnership

(US-AEP) and the GTN. US-AEP has placed environmental technology representatives in six Asian countries to identify trade opportunities for U.S. companies and coordinate meetings between potential Asian and U.S. business partners. These environmental trade specialists meet regularly with decision-makers in industry and government in order to prepare trade leads that identify Asian buyers, environmental concerns, and proposed technology solutions. These leads are forwarded to ETNA, where they are matched against a database of more than 5,000 registered U.S. companies and then e-mailed to those companies that provide the requested product or service.

Contact: For more information about ETNA, call (202) 835-0333, fax (202) 835-0446, e-mail *etna@usaep.org*, or visit *www.usgtn.net*.

Trade Mission OnLine, Small Business Administration

Trade Mission OnLine is a searchable database of U.S. small businesses that wish to export their products for use by foreign firms and U.S. businesses seeking U.S. partners or suppliers for trade-related activity. The database is designed to facilitate international small business sales, franchising, joint ventures, and licensing. The Trade Mission OnLine program is also used by SBA to recruit and provide time-sensitive trade promotion information to registered companies.

Contact: Find out more about or register with Trade Mission OnLine at *www.sba.gov/tmonline*. You can also contact the U.S. Small Business Administration, Office of International Trade, (202) 205-6720, fax (202) 205-7272, or home page *www.sba.gov/oit*.

ELECTRONIC AND PUBLISHED MARKET INFORMATION

Export.gov

Export.gov is the U.S. government's one-stop portal for current and potential U.S. exporters. Export.gov consolidates export program and foreign market intelligence across 19 federal agencies and presents it under one, easy-to-use Web site. Companies new to exporting can be guided step-by-step through the export process, and U.S. companies already exporting can view other guides, reference foreign tariff and tax information, search foreign and domestic trade events, subscribe to receive trade leads and industry-specific market intelligence, and gain access to federal export assistance and financing programs. Whether a company is exploring the possibility of entering foreign markets, searching for trade partners, seeking information on markets, or dealing with trade problems, Export.gov is the place to start. Additionally, the site links to federal sources of trade statistics, export documentation, financing, export licensing information, and much more.

Contact: Access the Web site at *www.export.gov*.

Trade and Industry Information, MAS, ITA, U.S. Department of Commerce

Comprehensive U.S. foreign trade and related international economic data useful in market research and evaluating trends in U.S. exports and imports by major product categories and foreign markets are provided by the Office of Trade and Industry Information (OTII). OTII supports the data needs of U.S. trade negotiators as well as U.S. companies and organizations involved in exporting. The OTII Web site includes national trade and industry statistics, state and local trade data, and links to key foreign country data sources.

Contact: For more information contact William Kolarik at (202) 482-4691, fax (202) 482-4614, or e-mail *William_Kolarik@ita.doc.gov*. The Web site address is *www.trade.gov/tradestats*.

Video Market Reports & Tutorial, CS, ITA, U.S. Department of Commerce

Video Market Reports & Tutorial consists of interactive international business Web casts, market briefs, and presentations in which in-country experts from the U.S. Commercial Service share their unique perspectives and identify new export opportunities for markets around the world.

Contact: Find the service at *www.export.gov*.

STAT-USA Electronic Information Products, U.S. Department of Commerce

STAT-USA

STAT-USA is the federal government's premier program for the publication of market information, trade leads, and other trade-related data, including the following electronic products:

- **STAT-USA/Internet.** Trade, economic, and business information is available on the Internet at *www.stat-usa.gov*. Thousands of international market reports and U.S. economic indicators from more than 40 different federal agencies are at your fingertips in an easy-to-navigate, on-line database. STAT-USA/Internet provides current business trade and procurement leads, timely economic statistics, and valuable international resources and contacts all in one convenient location. Information that would take hours to compile individually is now available in minutes. Subscriptions to STAT-USA/Internet are $75 for three months or $175 for a year of unlimited access. STAT-USA/Internet may also be accessed at no charge at more than 1,100 federal depository libraries nationwide.
- **USA Trade *Online*.** How many parachutes does the United States export to France? How many circuit boards does the United States import, and what percentage comes from Asia? USA Trade *Online* can tell you. This service provides U.S. import and export statistics for more than 18,000 commodities traded worldwide and the most current merchandise trade statistics available in a dynamic spreadsheet format. Using the statistics generated by the Foreign Trade Division of the U.S. Census Bureau and available through STAT-USA, USA Trade *Online* offers immediate delivery of the current and historical numbers 24 hours a day and the ability to manipulate data, store queries, and make charts. USA Trade *Online* is available on the Internet at $75 per month or $300 for an annual subscription. Call 800-STAT-USA

(800-782-8872) or (202) 482-1986, fax (202) 482-2164, or subscribe on-line at *www.usatradeon line.gov*. To find a federal depository library near you, view *www.gpoaccess.gov/libraries.html*.

- **EuroTrade *Online*.** Looking for import and export statistics to help you analyze the European market? Check out EuroTrade *Online*, the official European foreign trade statistics from Europe's authoritative statistical agency, EuroStat, in a dynamic new format previously unavailable to the American business community. EuroTrade *Online* allows you to access the European Union's ComExt (Commerce Extérieur) data series. You will find import and export data for 25 major European countries and more than 12,000 commodities up to the eight-digit European Harmonized System classification level. EuroTrade *Online* is available on the internet through STAT-USA at $1,015 per month or $2,900 for an annual subscription. Call 800-STAT-USA (800-782-8872) or (202) 482-1986, fax (202) 482-2164, or subscribe on-line at *www.eurotradeonline.gov*.

Country Commercial Guides, CS, ITA, U.S. Department of Commerce

Country Commercial Guides (CCGs), produced by the U.S. Commercial Service, provide overviews for doing business in more than 120 countries, including information about market conditions, best export prospects, export financing, distributors, and legal and cultural issues.

Contact: Find the CCGs at *www.export.gov*, or call a CS trade specialist at 800-USA-TRAD(E) (800-872-8723).

National Technical Information Service, U.S. Department of Commerce

The National Technical Information Service (NTIS) is a source for government-sponsored U.S. and global scientific, technical, engineering, and business information. NTIS offers a wide variety of export and international trade resources, including the official *Export Administration Regulations Manual* in paper copy, on CD, and at *www.ntis.gov/products/types/databases/export-regulations.asp*; the U.S. Trade Regulations at *www.ntis.gov/products/trade-regulations.asp*; and the Country Commercial Guides.

Contact: Call the NTIS Sales Desk at 800-553-NTIS (800-553-6847) or (703) 605-6000. The NTIS home page is *www.ntis.gov*.

International Data Base, U.S. Census Bureau, U.S. Department of Commerce

The International Programs Center compiles and maintains up-to-date global demographic and social information for all countries in its International Data Base (IDB), which is available to U.S. companies seeking to identify potential markets overseas.

Contact: To learn more about the IDB, contact Peter Johnson or Pat Dickerson, Information Resources Branch, at (301) 763-1351; fax (301) 457-1539; or e-mail *idb@census.gov*. Information about the IDB, including on-line access and free downloading, is available on the Internet at *www.census.gov/ipc/www/idbnew.html*.

Export and Import Trade Statistics, U.S. Census Bureau, U.S. Department of Commerce

U.S. export and import statistics by commodity, country, customs district, and method of transportation provide value and quantity on monthly, year-to-date, and annual history basis. Various levels of commodity classification, including the Harmonized System of Commodity Classification, Standard International Trade Classification, North American Industry Classification System, and end-use classification are available. U.S. state export data and port statistics for imports and exports are available. Tabulations, reports, and data files can be prepared to user specifications. Prices vary depending on user requirements and job size. Export and import statistics can be purchased on DVD for $1,200 a year, $500 a quarter, or $150 a month. U.S. merchandise trade data is available on-line at *www.usatradeonline.gov.*

Contact: For more information, call Vanessa Ware, Data Dissemination Branch, at (301) 457-2311; fax (301) 457-4615; or e-mail *ftd.data.dissemination@census.gov.* Contact Census Customer Service at (301) 763-4636 for DVDs, or visit the Foreign Trade Division's home page at *www.census.gov/foreign-trade/www.*

SBA Internet, Small Business Administration

The SBA home page provides SBA services, downloadable files, services from agency resource partners, links to other federal and state governments, and direct connections to additional outside resources. Special areas of interest focus on assisting U.S. small companies that are establishing new operations, seeking financing, looking to expand, and beginning to engage in exporting. The SBA home page also contains information on SBA programs that assist minority- and women-owned businesses. In addition, large libraries of business-focused shareware, downloadable SBA loan forms, and agency publications are available. A wide variety of services listed by state is provided, including local training courses sponsored by SBA. On-line workshops are offered for individuals to work through self-paced activities that help them start and expand their businesses. In addition, the home page links directly to the White House home page and the U.S. Business Advisor, which contain a large volume of regulatory information for small businesses. The SBA site provides full-text search capabilities as well as an area for user comments and suggestions.

Contact: Call the SBA Help Desk at (202) 205-6400. The SBA home page is at *www.sba.gov.*

Foreign Labor Trends, U.S. Department of Labor

Foreign Labor Trends (FLT) is a series of annual reports that describes and analyzes labor trends in selected countries. The reports are a comprehensive summary of host countries' labor institutions, practices, and key recent developments. The 2005 FLT report contains information assessing progress made by countries in complying with internationally recognized worker rights required for bilateral or regional free trade agreements.

Contact: For more information, call Sudha K. Haley, Office of Foreign Relations, at (202) 693-4801; fax (202) 693-4784; or e-mail *haley-sudha@dol.gov.*

CHAPTER 5

MAKING CONTACTS THROUGH TRADE PROMOTION EVENTS

DOMESTIC TRADE PROMOTION EVENTS

U.S. Export Pavilion

The U.S. Export Pavilion is a multi–U.S. government agency trade show exhibit that promotes the benefit of exporting and of using U.S. government export assistance. Participating agencies include the Foreign Trade Division of the U.S. Census Bureau, the U.S. Department of Commerce's Commercial Service, the Export–Import Bank, and the Small Business Administration. In addition to these U.S. government agencies, the National Customs Brokers and Forwarders Association of America also participates by helping companies find a customs broker or freight forwarder in their area. Together, these participants focus on export education and on helping U.S. companies to

- Research export markets
- Find international buyers
- Comply with export regulations
- Finance international buyers
- Ship products overseas

Contact: For information on the U.S. Export Pavilion, contact the Marketing and Communications Office of the U.S. Commercial Service at (202) 482-0581.

Regional Promotions, CS, ITA, U.S. Department of Commerce

A number of Web sites provide regional information:

- **Asia Now.** Asia Now's Web site brings together the resources of U.S. Commercial Service offices in 14 Asia–Pacific markets and of U.S. Export Assistance Centers throughout the United States. The Web site provides companies with a single point of access to regional trade events, extensive services, and research covering Asian markets. The home page is *www.buyusa.gov/asianow/*.
- **Access Eastern Mediterranean.** The Access Eastern Mediterranean Web site provides U.S. companies with maximum exposure in the region's markets and with its 180 million consumers. The unified promotion events target each of five broadly defined "best prospect" industries in Egypt, Israel, Jordan, Morocco, Lebanon, Turkey, and West Bank and the Gaza Strip. The home page is *www.buyusa.gov/easternmed/*.

- **The Americas.** The Americas Web site brings together the resources of U.S. Commercial Service offices in 21 markets throughout the region, providing companies with a single point of access to regional trade events, extensive services, and research covering markets throughout the region. The Americas Web site also provides information on the existing and proposed free trade agreements throughout the region, market research, best prospects in the region, trade event lists, industry-specific information, business service providers, useful links, and key contacts. The home page is *www.buyusa.gov/americas/.*
- **Showcase Europe.** The Showcase Europe Web site provides a framework for coordination and cooperation among the U.S. Department of Commerce's CS offices throughout Europe. Organized around eight key sectors (aerospace, automotive, energy and power generation, environmental technologies, information and communication technologies, medical and pharmaceutical, safety and security, and travel and tourism), Showcase Europe provides market briefing and counseling at major trade shows through a team of market and industry specialists from the U.S. Commercial Service. Technical assistance focuses on identifying specific high-potential export markets for U.S. participants. There is no fee for U.S. trade event participants. The home page is *www.buyusa.gov/europe/.*

Contact: For more information on regional promotions, contact your local U.S. Export Assistance Center. For the address and phone number of the USEAC nearest you, see Appendix A.

International Buyer Program, CS, ITA, U.S. Department of Commerce

The International Buyer Program (IBP) of the U.S. Commercial Service brings thousands of qualified international buyers and prospective distributors and trade partners to the United States each year to meet with U.S. companies at 28 major trade-only exhibitions. Without having to leave the country, U.S. exhibitors obtain worldwide promotion of their products and services and networking and matchmaking programs by country and industry experts.

Contact: For more information about the IBP, call Jim Boney, Global Trade Programs, at (202) 482-0146; fax (202) 482-0872; or e-mail *jim.boney@mail.doc.gov.* The home page is *www.export.gov.*

FOREIGN TRADE PROMOTION EVENTS

Overseas Trade Fair Certification, CS, ITA, U.S. Department of Commerce

Each year the U.S. Commercial Service certifies a limited number of private trade show organizers to recruit and manage U.S. pavilions at approximately 90 overseas trade shows worldwide. These private–public cooperative arrangements allow the organizers and the CS to combine and focus their support resources and expertise on selected events. Certification ensures that U.S. exhibiting firms are well briefed on the market, that the show and show organizer provide an excellent export marketing venue for the U.S. exhibitors, that the show and U.S. pavilion meet high standards, that there is a well located and high-visibility U.S. pavilion at the show, that exhibitors have complete CS support from U.S. embassies, and that firms that are new to exporting or to the market are exposed to appropriate buyers.

Contact: For information on the trade fair certification program, call 800-USA-TRAD(E) (800-872-8723), or visit *www.export.gov.*

Trade Fairs and Exhibitions, CS, ITA, U.S. Department of Commerce

In addition to certified shows, foreign and U.S. organizers produce many other good industry fairs of interest to U.S. exporters. The CS staff at U.S. embassies can identify these shows, arrange for participation, assist U.S. firms with market information, recommend pre- and post-event logistical and transportation support, and help exhibitors and visitors locate agents, distributors, and other potential buyers. Participation fees depend on the country and the show.

Contact: For information on trade show activities and a listing of all types of trade events, call the CS at 800-USA-TRAD(E) (800-872-8723), or view the trade events calendar on-line at *www.export.gov/tradeevents.html.*

Trade Missions, ITA, U.S. Department of Commerce

Trade missions are an essential element of a broad-based public program designed to increase job opportunities for all Americans. The U.S. Department of Commerce offers several types of trade missions:

- **Commercial missions.** These missions seek to produce near-term export sales of U.S. goods and services from participating firms that travel as a group to one or more foreign markets. Appointments are made with officials and prospective business partners and customers. Commercial missions are organized for individual sectors or multiple industries and may include a range of companies. Some missions are planned specifically for small and medium-sized firms or minority- and women-owned businesses.
- **Market access missions.** These missions seek to create commercial opportunities through the removal of trade barriers and opening of markets for U.S. businesses that have been closed out of such opportunities.
- **Policy missions.** These missions seek to advance U.S. bilateral or multilateral objectives across a range of issues, with the objective of enhancing overall bilateral or multilateral economic and political relations. This category includes missions designed to promote political stability in a foreign country or region by fostering U.S. investment and trade.
- **Combined missions.** These missions embody aspects of two or more of the above types.

- **Certified trade missions.** These missions are organized by state and private-sector trade promotion groups and supported by the U.S. Department of Commerce. States, industry associations, and other groups should apply directly to a Department of Commerce overseas post to have their mission certified.

Contact: To find information on all missions, visit the trade events calendar at *www.export.gov/tradeevents.html.*

Product Literature Centers, Sample Displays, and International Catalog Exhibition Program, CS, ITA, U.S. Department of Commerce

The Product Literature Centers and Sample Displays, which are part of the U.S. Commercial Service, are industry-focused exhibits at trade shows where knowledgeable Department of Commerce industry or trade specialists or U.S. embassy officials display U.S. company literature and samples to hundreds of interested business prospects. Sales leads are sent directly to participating companies. At International Catalog Exhibitions, state development agencies collaborate with the CS to showcase product literature from companies in their state and send trade leads to the participating U.S. firms.

Contact: For more information on Product Literature Centers, Sample Displays, and International Catalog Exhibitions, contact the CS at 800-USA-TRAD(E) (800-872-8723), or visit *www.export.gov/tradeevents.html.*

CHAPTER 6

SPECIAL MARKET ACCESS AND TECHNICAL ASSISTANCE

Advocacy and Multilateral Development Bank Center, CS, ITA, U.S. Department of Commerce

For U.S. companies bidding on foreign government project and procurement contracts, exporting means more than just selling a good product or service at a competitive price. It also means dealing with foreign governments and complex rules. If a bidding process for a contract is not open and transparent, or if it is tilted in favor of non-U.S. competitors, then contact the Advocacy and Multilateral Developmental Bank (AMDB) Center. The AMDB Center organizes and coordinates the actions of 19 U.S. government agencies to level the playing field on behalf of U.S. exporters and to ensure that sales of U.S. products and services have the best possible prospects abroad. The AMDB Center works with businesses of every size to develop targeted advocacy strategies and to craft appropriate advocacy messages for delivery to senior foreign officials and decision-makers. Additional advocacy assistance may include direct support supplied by U.S. embassy or consulate officials, U.S. export credit agency financing support to qualified U.S. companies, letters to foreign project decision-makers from senior U.S. officials, and other coordinated actions by U.S. government agencies.

Contact: For more information, call AMDB at (202) 482-3896, fax (202) 482-3508, visit *www.export.gov/advocacy*, or call the CS at 800-USA-TRAD(E) (800-872-8723).

Market Access and Compliance, ITA, U.S. Department of Commerce

The Market Access Compliance (MAC) unit works to open foreign markets for American goods and services, country by country and region by region, by working with U.S. exporters to overcome foreign trade barriers and develop strategies to level the playing field. MAC specialists maintain in-depth knowledge of the trade policies and practices of our trading partners. Working hand-in-hand with U.S. businesses, trade associations, and other U.S. government offices, MAC country and regional experts develop information needed to conduct trade negotiations, monitor foreign country compliance with trade agreements, and ensure that U.S. firms know how to use market opening agreements.

Contact: For appropriate contacts in MAC offices, call 800-USA-TRAD(E) (800-872-8723), or visit the home page at *www.mac.doc.gov*.

Trade Compliance Center, ITA, U.S. Department of Commerce

The Trade Compliance Center (TCC) ensures vigorous enforcement of existing U.S. international trade agreements. The TCC is a one-stop shop for U.S. businesses and industries concerned with foreign compliance with trade obligations, standards of behavior, or related problems with exporting. The TCC monitors, investigates, and evaluates foreign compliance with multilateral and bilateral trade agreements.

The TCC has the U.S. government's only comprehensive, free, and searchable Internet database of trade agreements and market-specific export information. This Web site assists new and experienced exporters in understanding their rights and their trading partners' obligations, as found in more than 300 trade agreements (including the World Trade Organization agreements and NAFTA). The Web site also provides direct access to the TCC through its "trade complaint hotline." One e-mail or fax to the TCC connects you to U.S. government trade policy assistance in resolving market access and trade agreement–related difficulties.

Contact: To contact the Trade Compliance Center, call (202) 482-1191 or fax (202) 482-6097. The Web site is *www.export.gov/tcc*.

ATA Carnet, U.S. Customs and Border Protection, U.S. Department of Homeland Security

The ATA Carnet is a special international customs document that may be used for temporary imports and exports, particularly professional equipment and commercial samples that are sent out of the country for less than one year. The carnet is issued in lieu of the usual customs documents and eliminates value added taxes, duties, and temporary import bonds. Seventy-five participating countries or territories accept the carnet as a guarantee against the payment of customs duties.

Contact: The issuing authority for the carnet is the United States Council for International Business, ATA Carnet Department, 1212 Avenue of the Americas, New York, NY 10036. Call (866) 786-5625 or (212) 703-5078, fax (212) 944-0012, e-mail *atacarnet@uscib.org*, or visit *www.uscib.org*. Additional information is available from the U.S. Customs and Border Protection, Office of Field Operations, 1300 Pennsylvania Ave., NW, Washington, DC 20229; (202) 344-1620. The Web site is *www.cbp.gov*.

Export Trade Certificate of Review Program, ITA, U.S. Department of Commerce

Under this program, U.S. firms can team up to gain economies of scale and share export costs and risks. The Certificate of Review offers antitrust preclearance on virtually any export activity, including joint negotiation with providers of export services regarding issues such as (1) reduced shipping rates, (2) agreements to sell together in export markets, (3) agreements to form coalitions to avoid rivalry in export markets, (4) coordination of export prices such as joint pricing, (5) joint bidding on projects, and (6) cost sharing on developing or expanding new export markets. This program provides firms with virtual immunity from antitrust liability at state and federal levels and significantly reduces their antitrust exposure at the private level.

Contact: To find out more about the program, call Export Trading Company Affairs at (202) 482-5131, or visit *www.ita.doc.gov/oetca*. To locate prospective U.S. export partners and export service firms, log on to *www.myexports.com*.

Office of the United States Trade Representative

Staff members at the Office of the U.S. Trade Representative (USTR) can provide information to exporters confronted with problems involving the implementation of international trade agreements. Offices are organized according to sectoral, functional, and geographic responsibilities.

Contact: For more information, contact the following USTR personnel: James Murphy, Agricultural Affairs, (202) 395-6127; Florizelle Liser, Office of African Affairs, (202) 395-9514; Christine Bliss, Services, Investment, and Intellectual Property Rights, (202) 395-4510; David Spooner, Office of Textiles, (202) 395-3026; and Meredith Broadbent, Office of Industry, (202) 395-5656. The fax for all offices is (202) 395-3911. The home page is *www.ustr.gov*.

Section 301 Relief, Office of the General Counsel, Office of the United States Trade Representative

The USTR is responsible for administering trade cases that provide relief from unfair trade practices under section 301 of the Trade Act of 1974. Individual exporters should contact the USTR concerning procedures for filing a complaint and defending U.S. interests and rights through the dispute settlement procedures of the World Trade Organization.

Contact: For section 301 assistance, contact Daniel Brinza, assistant U.S. trade representative for monitoring and enforcement, (202) 395-3582, or William Busis, chairman, Section 301 Committee, (202) 395-3150; fax (202) 395-3639.

National Center for Standards and Certification Information, National Institute of Standards and Technology, Technology Administration, U.S. Department of Commerce

The National Center for Standards and Certification Information (NCSCI) provides print and electronic resources on U.S. and foreign standards and standards-related information, technical regulations, and certification requirements. The center operates an "Export Alert!" service to inform subscribed parties via e-mail notifications of new regulations or changes to existing regulations for specific industry sectors and World Trade Organization countries. NCSCI also assists U.S. exporters in identifying standards and directives for products to be marketed internationally. NCSCI is the U.S. inquiry point for the World Trade Organization's Agreement on Technical Barriers to Trade, for the North American Free Trade Agreement, and for the International Organization for Standardization Information Network.

Contact: For more information, call the National Center for Standards and Certification Information at (301) 975-4040, fax (301) 926-1559, e-mail *ncsci@nist.gov*, or visit *www.ts.nist.gov/ncsci/*. Individuals may register for "Export Alert!" on-line at *http://ts.nist.gov/export-alert/*.

Laws and Metric Group, National Institute of Standards and Technology, Technology Administration, U.S. Department of Commerce

The Laws and Metric Group provides guidance related to packaging and labeling requirements, net content requirements, and the use of the metric system of measurement with the goal of making U.S. packaged goods more competitive in the export market and eliminating technical barriers to trade. The group also furnishes sources of information on metric standards and requirements in export markets.

Contact: To learn more, call Kenneth S. Butcher, group leader, at (301) 975-4859, fax (301) 926-0647, e-mail *TheSI@nist.gov*, or visit *www.nist.gov/metric*.

Bureau of Economic and Business Affairs, U.S. Department of State

The Bureau of Economic and Business Affairs integrates high-level economic expertise in areas such as international trade and investment policy, finance, telecommunications and information technology, energy and sanctions, international transportation issues, agriculture, and intellectual property rights with up-to-date information about economic and other developments around the world to advance U.S. interests. The Office of Commercial and Business Affairs, which is part of the Bureau of Economic and Business Affairs, works directly with U.S. business representatives to help them tap into the worldwide resources of the State Department. It also champions U.S. business interests overseas with outreach, advocacy, troubleshooting, and market access support and engages business leaders on strategic international issues that affect them.

Contact: You can call the Office of Commercial and Business Affairs at (202) 647-1625, fax (202) 647-3953, or visit *www.state.gov/e/eb/cba*. The Bureau of Economic and Business Affairs home page is *www.state.gov/e/eb*.

Office of Small and Disadvantaged Business Utilization, Minority Resource Center, U.S. Agency for International Development

U.S. small businesses and disadvantaged enterprises have an advocate that ensures their consideration as sources for the procurement of goods and services financed through USAID sustainable development activities. The Office of Small and Disadvantaged Business Utilization (OSDBU) maintains the Small Business Resource Database (SBRD), a fully automated, Web-based system by which small businesses can register with USAID. The SBRD is password protected for companies to enter and update their information, and, once registered, their capabilities can be accessed wherever USAID officers have Internet access. OSDBU has also published a guide to doing business with the Agency for International Development, *Creating Opportunities*, which is available in both English and Spanish and in hard copy or mini-CD disk format.

Contact: For more information, call Marilyn Marton, Office of Small and Disadvantaged Business Utilization, at (202) 712-1500, fax (202) 216-3056, or visit *www.usaid.gov/procurement_bus_opp/osdbu.*

Management and Technical Assistance Program, Office of Minority Enterprise Development, Small Business Administration

Through the Management and Technical Assistance Program, the SBA contracts for the services of professional management firms and others to provide help to section 8(a) and other eligible firms in the areas of accounting, marketing, proposal preparation, and industry-specific issues.

Contact: Additional information may be obtained from a business opportunity specialist in the SBA's district offices. For the phone and fax numbers of your nearest SBA district office, call 800-U-ASK-SBA (800-827-5722). The home page is *www.sba.gov/8abd.*

Overseas Security Advisory Council, U.S. Department of State

The Overseas Security Advisory Council (OSAC) is a joint venture between the State Department and the U.S. private sector to interact on overseas security problems, such as political unrest, crime, terrorism, and protection of sensitive information. The OSAC maintains a continuing liaison between security officials in both the private and public sectors, provides for regular exchanges of information on emerging threats and developments in protective security, and recommends methods for planning and implementing security programs abroad to protect the competitiveness of American businesses operating worldwide. The OSAC works closely with U.S. embassies and consulates to address global security concerns and facilitate coordination between the State Department's Bureau of Diplomatic Security, U.S. business representatives, and regional security officers at diplomatic missions abroad. OSAC, through its Country Council program, provides a highly effective forum for embassy security officials and private-sector organizations to share security concerns, threat-related information, and best practices. The OSAC Web site provides unclassified analytical products, country-specific updates, and comprehensive and timely security- and threat-related information.

Contact: To find out more, call the OSAC at (571) 345-2214, fax (571) 345-2238, or visit *www.ds-osac.org*.

Workshops and Conferences, U.S. Trade and Development Agency

The U.S. Trade and Development Agency (USTDA) organizes workshops, conferences, and technical symposia worldwide. These events are sector or project oriented and are aimed at connecting overseas project sponsors with U.S. firms and entities that supply project finance, technology, and industry expertise that may be useful in project implementation. USTDA contracts with prequalified professional conference specialists to organize these activities.

Contact: For more information, call the USTDA Information Resource Center at (703) 875-4357, fax (703) 875-4009, e-mail *info@ustda.gov*, or visit *www.ustda.gov*.

CHAPTER 7

EXPORT FINANCE, INSURANCE, AND GRANTS (NON-AGRICULTURAL)

EXPORT FINANCE

Export–Import Bank of the United States

Ex–Im Bank provides a variety of export finance assistance, including export credit insurance, pre-export financing through working capital guaranteed loans to exporters, and medium- and long-term loans and guarantees to overseas buyers. Ex–Im Bank offers various programs to the business community, including regular seminars and group briefings at several locations around the country. Specific Ex–Im Bank programs are described below.

Contact: For information on all Ex–Im Bank programs, call the export financing hotline at (800) 565-EXIM (800-565-3946), or, for Alaska, Hawaii, and the District of Columbia, (202) 565-3946. Fax retrieval is available at (800) 565-EXIM, press 1, press 2. Send e-mails to *bdd@exim.gov*. The home page is *www.exim.gov*.

City–State Program, Export–Import Bank of the United States

Ex–Im Bank works with state and local government agencies to offer export counseling and financial assistance to businesses in their jurisdictions. Cooperative programs currently operate in more than 42 states and regions as well as in Puerto Rico.

Contact: To learn more about the City–State Program, call Gus Grace, business development officer, at (202) 565-3910 or fax (202) 565-3932.

Regional Offices, Export–Import Bank of the United States

Ex–Im Bank's regional offices provide services and information to businesses. Regional offices are in New York; Washington, D.C.; Miami; Chicago; Houston; Orange County, California; and Long Beach; San Diego, and San Francisco, California. Ex–Im Bank is also represented at most U.S. Export Assistance Centers.

Contact: The regional offices are as follows: *New York*: 20 Exchange Place, 40/F, New York, NY 10005, (212) 809-2650, fax (212) 809-2646; *Washington, D.C.*: 811 Vermont Avenue, NW, Room 929, Washington, DC 20571, (202) 565-3900, fax (202) 565-3931; *Miami*: 777 N.W. 72nd Avenue, Suite 3M2, Miami, FL 33126, (305) 526-7436, fax (305) 526-7435; *Chicago*: 200 West Adams Street, Suite 2450, Chicago, IL 60606, (312) 353-8040, fax (312) 353-8098; *Houston*:

1880 South Dairy, Ashford II, Suite 585, Houston, TX 77077, (281) 721-0465, fax (281) 679-0156; *Orange County, California*: 3300 Irvine Avenue, Suite 305, Newport Beach, CA 92660, (949) 660-1688 ext. 150, fax (949) 660-8039; *Long Beach, California*: 1 World Trade Center, Suite 1670, Long Beach, CA 90831, (562) 980-4580, fax (562) 980-4590; *San Diego, California*: 6363 Greenwich Drive, Suite 230, San Diego, CA 92122, (619) 557-7091, fax (619) 557-6176, *San Francisco, California*: 250 Montgomery Street, 14th Floor, San Francisco, CA 94104, (415) 705-2285, fax (415) 705-1156. For the addresses and phone numbers of USEACs, see Appendix A.

Working Capital Guarantee Program, Export–Import Bank of the United States

The Working Capital Guarantee Program helps small and medium-sized businesses obtain critical pre-export financing from commercial lenders. Ex–Im Bank guarantees 90 percent of the principal and interest on transaction-specific loans or revolving lines of credit that are extended to eligible exporters. The funds may be used for pre-export activities, which include the purchase of raw materials, labor, overhead, performance bonds, retainers, and warranties. Ex–Im Bank processes loan amounts of more than $833,333; lower amounts go to the Small Business Administration.

Contact: For more information about the Working Capital Guarantee Program, call Pamela Bowers at (202) 565-3792, fax (202) 565-3793, visit *www.exim.gov*, or contact an Ex–Im Bank regional office.

Export Credit Insurance, Export–Import Bank of the United States

Ex–Im Bank offers insurance policies that cover political and commercial risks on export receivables.

- **Small Business Policy.** This policy is available to firms just beginning to export or with average annual export credit sales of less than $5 million for the past two years. These businesses must also meet the Small Business Administration's definition of a small business. The policy offers enhanced coverage, a lower premium than usually found in other insurance policies, and an enhanced assignment used to discount receivables with a bank. Special features are also available for exporters of environmental goods and services.
- **Bank Letter of Credit Policy.** This policy insures commercial banks against loss on irrevocable letters of credit issued by foreign banks on behalf of importers purchasing U.S. goods and services.
- **Multi-Buyer Policy.** This policy insures all of an exporter's short-term export credit sales or a reasonable spread.
- **Financial Institution Buyer Credit Policy.** This policy insures individual short-term export credits extended by financial institutions to foreign buyers.
- **Short-Term Single-Buyer Policy** and the **Medium-Term Single-Buyer Policy.** These policies allow exporters to insure their receivables against loss attributable to commercial and specified political risks on a selective basis.

- **Lease Insurance Policies.** These policies offer a lessor the opportunity to expand its overseas leasing program by providing comprehensive insurance for both the stream of lease payments and the fair market value of the leased products.

Contact: For more information, call the Business Development Office, at (202) 565-3900, fax (202) 565-3931, visit *www.exim.gov*, or contact an Ex–Im Bank regional office.

Direct Loans and Guarantees, Export–Import Bank of the United States

This program extends direct loans to foreign buyers or extends guarantees to financing intermediaries for creditworthy entities that purchase U.S. capital goods or services. The loans and guarantees offered are for 85 percent of the U.S. export value. Direct loans provide competitive fixed-rate financing to the foreign buyer. The guarantee coverage provides protection to the source of finance against payment default for either political or commercial reasons. Interest rates for the guarantees are negotiated between the source of finance and the seller and are typically floating rates. Political-only guarantee coverage is also available. In addition, Ex–Im Bank is willing to provide support for a broad range of environmental exports, including special transaction structures for certain lease transactions, industrial design, architectural or engineering services, and overseas operations and maintenance contracts.

Contact: To learn more, call the Business Development Office, (202) 565-3900, fax (202) 565-3931, visit *www.exim.gov*, or contact an Ex–Im Bank regional office.

Limited Recourse Project Finance Program, Export–Import Bank of the United States

The Limited Recourse Project Finance Program provides financing for projects that depend on the cash flows of the project for repayment, not on recourse to a foreign government, financial institution, or established corporation. Combinations of direct loans, political risk–only coverage, or comprehensive guarantees for commercial bank loans are available. Ex–Im Bank now offers precompletion comprehensive coverage for selected projects. Ex–Im Bank offerings include financing up to 85 percent of the U.S. export value, financing of interest during construction, and financing of host-country local costs of up to 15 percent of the U.S. contract value and up to the maximum repayment terms consistent with the guidelines of the Organization for Economic Cooperation and Development.

Contact: For more information, call Kristine Wood at (202) 565-3913, fax (202) 565-3695, or visit *www.exim.gov*.

Small Business Administration

SBA finances the short-term and cyclical working-capital needs of small businesses and administers business loan programs to help qualified small businesses obtain financing. The financing programs and appropriate contacts listed below can help exporters.

Contact: The Web site for SBA is *www.sba.gov/financing.*

Business Loan Guarantee Program, Small Business Administration

SBA's 7(a) program assists qualified small businesses in obtaining financial assistance from banks. The Business Loan Guarantee Program provides the lender with a guarantee that, if the borrower cannot repay the loan, the federal government will repay it up to the percentage of SBA guarantee. Therefore, when a business applies for an SBA loan, it is applying for a commercial loan with an SBA guarantee.

SBA can make 7(a) loans to businesses engaged in manufacturing, construction, wholesale, retail, or service industries, and the proceeds may be used to acquire equipment, facilities, machinery, supplies, or materials; to obtain working capital; to finance construction, conversion, or expansion; and to refinance existing debt.

The maximum dollar amount that SBA will guarantee is $1.5 million. The maximum maturity is 25 years; however, SBA expects all loans to be repaid as soon as possible. Therefore, maturity is based on the ability of the business to pay without hardship. Interest rates on SBA guarantee loans are negotiated between the applicant and the lender on the basis of the credit merits of the request, subject to a maximum of the prime rate plus 2.75 percent.

Contact: Call (800) U-ASK-SBA (800-827-5722) for the nearest SBA district office or U.S. Export Assistance Center for an application, or go to *www.sba.gov/financing.*

SBA Export Finance, Small Business Administration

SBA Export Finance programs for small business exporters take the form of loan guarantees to participating lenders who provide the capital. There are three different programs briefly described below. For more information, visit the Web sites, or contact the SBA staff in the U.S. Export Assistance Centers.

For a listing, visit *www.sba.gov/oit/export/useac.*

Export Working Capital Program. The Export Working Capital Program (EWCP) loans provide transaction financing for small exporters. The loans can be structured to support financing for single transactions, export contracts, and lines of credit. The loan term is typically one year or less. Preshipment financing can cover materials, labor, and export-related costs; postshipment financing of the export receivables and stand-by letters of credit used as performance bond; and payment guarantee or bid bonds. With the co-guarantee agreement between SBA and Ex–Im Bank, EWCP loans can now be approved up to $2 million using one single application. The borrower must be a small business and have export sales, must have one year of business experience, and must agree to assign proceeds from export sales. Other conditions may apply. Interest rates and fees are negotiated between business and lender. Application information is available from U.S. Export Assistance Centers. See also *www.sba.gov/financing/loanprog/ewcp.*

International Trade Loan Program. International trade loans can be used to finance equipment and facilities or as working capital by companies that are new to export, exporters needing to expand, or companies adversely affected by import competition. Loan maturities can be up to 25 years, and loan maximums are the same as standard SBA loans. Application is made through SBA lenders. Interest rates and fees are negotiated between business and lender. For more information, see *www.sba.gov/financing/loanprog/tradeloans.*

Export Express Program. Export Express loans can finance a variety of export-related costs: market development (for trade shows, translation of product literature, and so forth); transaction financing; equipment for the production of goods to be exported; and stand-by letters of credit for bid and performance bonds or payment guarantees. The maximum loan amount is $350,000. Application for this loan is through SBA Express lenders, who are able to use their own forms, documentation, and approval process. To be eligible, small businesses must have been in business for one year and must plan to export. Interest rates and fees are negotiated between business and lender. Visit *www.sba.gov/financing/loanprog/exportexpress.*

Small Business Investment Companies, Small Business Administration

Small business investment companies (SBICs), licensed by the SBA, are privately owned and managed venture capital and investment firms. SBICs with investment strategies that include export activities may receive equity capital or term working capital in excess of the SBA's statutory limit.

Contact: To learn more about SBICs, call the Investment Division at (202) 205-6510, or visit *www.sba.gov/inv.*

Untied Aid Initiatives, ITA, U.S. Department of Commerce

Untied aid is financing provided by wealthier countries to developing countries and emerging markets for development projects. It is primarily provided in the form of concessional loans where procurement is not contingent on the purchase of goods and services from the donor country. Untied aid can offer U.S. firms significant business opportunities.

U.S. firms interested in pursuing procurement opportunities associated with untied aid-funded projects should familiarize themselves with the Organization for Economic Cooperation and Development (OECD), which provides information on projects financed with bilateral untied aid on two of its Web sites.

- The first is a new Web site maintained by the OECD's Export Credit Secretariat. In November 2004, 25 members of the OECD that are participants to the Export Credit

Arrangement agreed to a U.S. proposal to open the bidding process for projects in developing countries that are financed with untied aid credits. The two-year pilot agreement began on Jan. 1, 2005. For the first time, the agreement sets multilateral requirements for OECD governments to report publicly on the details of their untied aid–financed projects, including the outcome of each bid competition. The value of untied aid credits covered by this agreement has averaged more than $7 billion annually since 1995 and was as high as $14 billion in 1996. You should visit *http://webdomino1.oecd.org/comnet/dcd/untiedpubliccws.nsf.*

- The second one is the untied aid bulletin board of the OECD's Development Assistance Committee (DAC), *www.oecd.org/dac/.* It is based on a 2001 agreement to provide untied aid notifications for projects in the least developed countries.

Contact: For more information on untied aid initiatives, contact the following: Danius Barzdukas, Office of Japan, (202) 482-1147, fax (202) 482-0469, or e-mail *danius_barzdukas@ita.doc.gov*; Denise Carpenter, Office of Finance, (202) 482-4002, fax (202) 482-5702, or e-mail *denise_carpenter@ita.doc.gov.* You can also visit *http://web.ita.doc.gov/sif/untied.nsf/.*

Multilateral Development Bank Commercial Liaisons Advocacy and Multilateral Developmental Bank Center Trade Advocacy Center, CS, ITA, U.S. Department of Commerce

Multilateral Development Bank (MDB) commercial liaisons counsel U.S. firms about export opportunities associated with projects and procurements funded by the World Bank, the Asian Development Bank, the African Development Bank, the Inter-American Development Bank, and the European Bank for Reconstruction and Development. MDB liaison officers ensure project and procurement information is available on a timely basis and they organize, develop, and implement outreach programs throughout the United States. The development banks assist in financing social and economic infrastructure—as well as privatization—projects in developing countries. The U.S. liaison officers in each of these institutions are dedicated to the identification of these projects at the earliest possible stage. They provide in-depth counseling to U.S. firms on these project and procurement opportunities and advocate on behalf of U.S. commercial interests.

Contact: For more information, contact the following: World Bank, Commercial Liaison Office, (202) 458-0120, fax (202) 477-2967; Inter-American Development Bank, Commercial Liaison Office, (202) 623-3821, fax (202) 623-2039; African Development Bank, Commercial Liaison Office (Tunisia), +216-71-10-34-65, fax +216-71-10-37-62; Asian Development Bank, Commercial Liaison Office (Philippines), +632 887-1345 or 1346, fax +632 887-1164; European Bank for Recon-struction and Development (United Kingdom), +44 20-7588-8489 or 8490, fax +44 20-7588-8443. You can also call the Trade Information Center at (800) USA-TRAD(E) (800-872-8723).

INVESTMENT FINANCE

Overseas Private Investment Corporation

The Overseas Private Investment Corporation (OPIC) helps U.S. businesses invest overseas, fosters economic development in new and emerging markets, complements the private sector in managing risks associated with foreign direct investment, and supports U.S. foreign policy. Because OPIC charges market-based fees for its products, it operates on a self-sustaining basis at no net cost to taxpayers. OPIC promotes U.S. best practices by requiring that projects adhere to international standards on the environment, workers rights, and human rights.

Contact: To learn more, call the OPIC InfoLine at (202) 336-8799, fax (202) 408-9859, or visit *www.opic.gov*. Callers with a touchtone phone may listen to brief recorded program descriptions, request that printed program information be sent to them via mail or fax, or—from 8:45 a.m. to 5:30 p.m. EST—speak with an OPIC information officer.

Investment Insurance, Overseas Private Investment Corporation

OPIC offers several programs to insure U.S. investments in emerging markets and developing countries against the risks of (1) currency inconvertibility (the inability to convert profits, debt service, and other investment remittances from local currency into U.S. dollars or the inability to transfer funds); (2) expropriation (loss of an investment due to expropriation, nationalization, or confiscation by the host government); and (3) political violence (loss of assets or income because of war, revolution, insurrection, or politically motivated civil strife, terrorism, or sabotage). Coverage is available for new ventures, expansion of existing enterprises, privatizations, and acquisitions with positive developmental benefits. Coverage is available for equity investments, parent company and third-party loans and loan guarantees, technical assistance agreements, leases, consigned inventory or equipment, and other forms of investment.

Contact: For more information, call the OPIC InfoLine at (202) 336-8799, fax (202) 408-9859, or visit *www.opic.gov*.

Finance Programs, Overseas Private Investment Corporation

OPIC provides financing through direct loans and loan guarantees for medium- and long-term private investment. Loans range from $100,000 to $250 million for projects sponsored by U.S. companies, and financing can be provided on a project finance or corporate finance basis. In most cases, the U.S. sponsor is expected to contribute at least 25 percent of the project equity, have a track record in the industry, and have the means to contribute to the financial success of the project. For U.S. small businesses with annual revenues under $35 million, OPIC's Small Business Center can provide financing through a streamlined approval process and an "insurance wrap" that offers political risk insurance coverage at a reduced rate.

Additionally, to address the lack of sufficient equity investment in emerging markets, OPIC has supported the creation of privately owned and managed investment funds that make direct equity and equity-related investments in new, expanding, or privatizing companies.

Contact: To find out about finance programs, call the OPIC InfoLine at (202) 336-8799, fax (202) 408-9859, or visit *www.opic.gov.*

GRANTS AND FUNDING FOR FEASIBILITY STUDIES AND OTHER EXPORT-RELATED NEEDS

Feasibility Studies, U.S. Trade and Development Agency

USTDA provides grants for overseas infrastructure project planning assistance, such as feasibility studies. These studies evaluate the technical, financial, environmental, legal, and other critical aspects of infrastructure development projects that are of interest to potential lenders and investors. Host-country project sponsors select the U.S. companies, normally through open competitions, that perform USTDA-funded feasibility studies.

Contact: For more information, call the USTDA Information Resource Center at (703) 875-4357, fax (703) 875-4009, or e-mail *info@ustda.gov.* A model proposal format can be found on USTDA's Web site *www.ustda.gov.*

Technical Assistance Grants, U.S. Trade and Development Agency

USTDA provides technical assistance to help with the development of sector strategies, industry standards, and legal and regulatory regimes. This assistance helps create a favorable business and trade environment. Transportation safety and security are particularly important sectors for USTDA's technical assistance work.

Contact: To learn more about technical assistance grants, call the USTDA Information Resource Center at (703) 875-4357, fax (703) 875-4009, or e-mail *info@ustda.gov.* A model proposal format can be found on USTDA's Web site: *www.ustda.gov.*

Desk Studies and Definitional Missions, U.S. Trade and Development Agency

One of the earliest stages of project planning is the development of terms of reference for an activity that will define the technical, environmental, financial, and other factors that must be addressed before an investment decision can be made. USTDA helps ensure that a project is appropriately conceived by contracting with technical specialists to perform definitional missions and desk studies. These independent assessments develop the appropriate terms of reference and budget for pertinent project preparation activities. Using U.S. private-sector resources and expertise, these activities provide preliminary assessments of the economic viability of proposed projects and determine whether they meet USTDA's funding criteria.

Contact: Direct contracting opportunities with USTDA are posted on the Federal Business Opportunities Web site at *www.fedbizopps.gov.* Small businesses interested in providing USTDA with consultant services related to project evaluations should register with USTDA's On-Line Consultant Database at *www.ustda.gov* and with the federal government's Central Contractor Registration site at *www.ccr.gov.* Questions should be directed to USTDA's Information Resource Center, (703) 875-4357, fax (703) 875-4009, or e-mail *info@ustda.gov.*

Trust Funds at Multilateral Development Banks, U.S. Trade and Development Agency

USTDA maintains trust funds at four MDBs: the International Finance Corporation, the European Bank for Reconstruction and Development, Inter-American Development Bank, and the Inter-American Development Bank's private-sector arm, the Inter-American Investment Corporation. These funds, most of which are known as *evergreen funds*, can be used for technical assistance and feasibility studies. USTDA maintains a minimum balance that is readily available to fund project opportunities for U.S. firms or to help U.S. businesses take advantage of time-sensitive projects.

Since MDBs finance many of the capital projects in the developing world, USTDA's close relationship with them is advantageous for the U.S. business community. In addition to the valuable project information gained through the MDBs, which USTDA passes on to U.S. firms, working with bank projects ensures that a potential funding source has been identified.

Contact: Call the USTDA Information Resource Center at (703) 875-4357 and ask for the regional director for the country where a project is located, or fax Barbara Bradford, deputy director, at (703) 875-4009. You can also e-mail *info@ustda.gov* or visit *www.ustda.gov.*

Training Grants, U.S. Trade and Development Agency

USTDA provides training for foreign decision-makers in economic sectors where there are opportunities for the sale of U.S. equipment and services. The training is normally focused on technology or regulatory issues and is designed to give project sponsors a better understanding of U.S. experience and capabilities. Training can be conducted in the United States or in the host country.

Contact: To learn more about training grants, call the USTDA Information Resource Center at (703) 875-4357, fax (703) 875-4009, e-mail *info@ustda.gov*, or visit *www.ustda.gov.*

Market Development Cooperator Program Grants, ITA, U.S. Department of Commerce

The MDCP is a competitive matching funds program operated by the International Trade Administration. The program builds public-private partnerships by providing federal assistance to non-profit export multipliers such as states, trade associations, chambers of commerce, and small business development centers. These multipliers can be particularly effective in helping small and medium-sized enterprises to be more competitive. Applicants use their own creativity to design projects that will help such enterprises enter, expand, or maintain market share in targeted markets abroad. MDCP awards help underwrite the start-up costs of new foreign market development ventures.

Contact: To find out more about the program, call the MDCP program manager at (202) 482-2969, or visit *www.export.gov/mdcp*.

Special American Business Internship Training, ITA, U.S. Department of Commerce

The Special American Business Internship Training (SABIT) Program is a public-private joint initiative to promote market access and to cultivate economic and civil society development in Eurasia: Armenia, Azerbaijan, Belarus, Georgia, Kazakhstan, Kyrgyzstan, Moldova, Russia, Tajikistan, Turkmenistan, Ukraine, and Uzbekistan. SABIT offers grant funding to American companies and organizations and provides group training programs for Eurasian professionals. These training programs balance the technical assistance needs of Eurasia's emerging markets with the interests of the U.S. business and scientific communities. SABIT grants, available to any American company, non-governmental organization, or academic institution, cover a share of the costs incurred in hosting Eurasian managers and scientists for three to six months of hands-on professional training in a U.S. business setting. Since 1990, SABIT has enabled more than 1,000 organizations to host more than 3,300 trainees. With funding of $47 million to date, SABIT is a leading technical assistance provider driving public-private partnerships between the U.S. and Eurasian scientific and business communities.

Contact: To learn more about the SABIT Program, call (202) 482-0073, fax (202) 482-2443, or visit *www.mac.doc.gov/sabit*.

EcoLinks Partnership Grants Program, Institute for International Education, U.S. Agency for International Development

EcoLinks, the Eurasian–American Partnership for Environmentally Sustainable Economies, is a USAID-funded program that promotes market-based solutions to urban and industrial environmental problems in Central and Eastern Europe and Eurasia. EcoLinks provides grants and facilitates trade and investment to create lasting environmentally focused partnerships between businesses, local governments, and relevant associations in the region and their counterparts in the United States. The EcoLinks grants program provides Quick Response Awards, up to $5,000 each, to support travel-related partnering activities such as meetings and site visits and identifies industry best practices to be used as models for future development in the region.

Contact: For more information, call Ioana Hartshorn, program officer, EcoLinks Partnership Grant Program, at (202) 326-7814, fax (202) 326-7774, e-mail *ihartshorn@iie.org*, or visit *www.ecolinks.org*.

Office of Citizen Exchanges, U.S. Department of State

The U.S. Department of State designs and develops exchange programs to encourage market-based economic development. It funds programs conducted by U.S. non-profit organizations that work with international leaders, including young professionals and business entrepreneurs. Open, merit-based competitions are conducted annually for proposals on specific themes in specific regions worldwide.

Contact: For more information, call the Office of Citizen Exchanges at (202) 619-5348, fax (202) 619-4350, or visit *http://exchanges.state.gov*.

CHAPTER 8

AGRICULTURAL EXPORT AND FINANCE PROGRAMS

AGRICULTURAL EXPORT PROGRAMS

FAS Worldwide, Foreign Agricultural Service, U.S. Department of Agriculture

FAS Worldwide is a quarterly magazine that covers the full spectrum of FAS responsibilities on a worldwide basis, including market access, market development, and foreign policy. Introduced in Spring 2005, it replaces the monthly publication AgExporter.

Contact: For subscription information, call the National Technical Information Service at (703) 605-6060 (Washington, D.C., area) or (800) 999-6779 (toll free). To view FAS Worldwide, go to the FAS home page at *www.fas.usda.gov*.

Processed Products Division, Foreign Agricultural Service, U.S. Department of Agriculture

The AgConnections team of the Processed Products Division manages five basic services that are available to exporters of U.S. food, farm, forest, fish, and seafood products:

- *Trade leads* are foreign trade inquiries that the FAS offices transmit electronically to the USDA. They are made available to U.S. exporters via e-mail free of charge. Trade leads are also available through trade publications and state departments of agriculture and trade development centers. Contact Sharon Claggett at (202) 690-3416.
- *Buyer Alert* is a biweekly newsletter that can introduce your food, farm, forest, fish, and seafood products to foreign buyers at only $15 per announcement. Advertisements for up to five products may be submitted for each announcement every eight weeks. *Buyer Alert* announcements are transmitted electronically directly to more than 17,000 potential buyers in more than 85 countries. Contact Linda Conrad at (202) 690-3421.
- *Foreign buyer lists* contain detailed contact information on more than 26,000 importers of food, farm, forest, and seafood products in 80 countries. Lists may be ordered by product or by country at a cost of $15 each. Contact Sharon Claggett at (202) 690-3416.
- *U.S. supplier lists* may be used to source U.S. food, farm, forest, fish, and seafood products for export. Qualified U.S. companies that are export ready can register on-line to be included in the U.S. Suppliers List Database. U.S. companies must have a Dun & Bradstreet number to register. Contact Linda Conrad at (202) 690-3421.

- *The Export Directory of U.S. Food Distribution Companies* provides detailed information on U.S. suppliers of mixed containers of grocery or food service products to foreign buyers. Registration is free of charge. Contact Anne Almond at (202) 690-2853.

Contact: For further assistance, call the Processed Products Division at (202) 720-6343, fax (202) 690-4374, e-mail *agexport@fas.usda.gov*, or visit *www.fas.usda.gov/agexport/exporter.html.*

National Agricultural Library, U.S. Department of Agriculture

The National Agricultural Library (NAL) is a repository of information on agricultural marketing and trade. The NAL staff responds to inquiries with customized assistance by combining in-depth knowledge of the library's resources, state-of-the-art technology, and networking. The NAL staff also assists users in accessing the library's on-line catalog and article citation database, AGRICOLA (Agricultural On-line Access database).

Contact: To learn more, call the NAL Service Desk at (301) 504-5755, fax (301) 504-6110, or e-mail *agref@nal.usda.gov*. The National Agricultural Library home page is *www.nal.usda.gov*, and the AGRICOLA home page is *http://agricola.nal.usda.gov/*.

Economic Research Service, U.S. Department of Agriculture

The Economic Research Service (ERS) provides in-depth economic analyses on agricultural economies, trade policies of foreign countries, world agricultural trade and development issues, and their links with the U.S. food and fiber economy. The ERS analyzes how factors influencing demand (population, income, and tastes); production variables (inputs and technology); foreign governments' commercial policies and programs (price controls, environmental and food safety laws, and tariffs); macroeconomic conditions (exchange rates and debt); and major events (for example, China's accession to the World Trade Organization) affect countries' agricultural production, consumption, and trade; international food and fiber prices; and U.S. food and fiber competitiveness. The ERS widely disseminates information and analyses on international agricultural trade, food aid, and development through regional and commodity reports, bulletins and updates, periodicals, and electronic databases.

Contact: For more information, call Cheryl Christensen, deputy director, Market and Trade Economics Division at (202) 694-5203, fax (202) 694-5792, or e-mail *cherylc@ers.usda.gov*. The ERS home page is *www.ers.usda.gov*.

Trade Shows and Missions, Foreign Agricultural Service, U.S. Department of Agriculture

The USDA Trade Show Office offers U.S. food and beverage exporters a choice of programs to satisfy their marketing needs. Programs include fully sponsored trade shows, sales missions, endorsed shows in both leading and emerging markets worldwide, and American cafés. Fully sponsored trade shows consist of a package of services, including a fully appointed booth, shipping of product samples, and educational programs. Sales missions include guaranteed appointments with potential buyers, orientation to the market, and translation services. In addition, the USDA Trade Show Office provides information on the promoters of other international food and beverage shows.

Contact: For more information, call the USDA Trade Show Office at (202) 690-1182, fax (202) 690-4374, or visit *www.fas.usda.gov*.

Rural Development, Cooperative Services, U.S. Department of Agriculture

This program researches cooperative involvement in international trade and provides trade-related technical assistance to U.S. farmer-owned cooperatives.

Contact: To learn more, call Tracey Kennedy, International Trade Program at (202) 690-1428, fax (202) 690-2723, or e-mail *tracey.kennedy@usda.gov*. The home page is *www.rurdev.usda.gov/rbs/coops/csdir.htm*.

AGRICULTURAL TECHNICAL ASSISTANCE

Transportation Services, Agricultural Marketing Service, U.S. Department of Agriculture

As a USDA authority on transporting agricultural products to market, the Transportation Services Branch (TSB) informs, represents, and assists agricultural shippers. Activities include

- Market reports
- Regulatory representation
- Economic analysis and reports
- Technical assistance
- Outreach
- Responding to inquiries

Contact: To learn more, call the TSB staff at (202) 690-1304, fax (202) 690-3616, or visit *www.ams.usda.gov/tmd/tsb*.

Shipper Assistance, Agricultural Marketing Service, U.S. Department of Agriculture

The Office of Shipper and Exporter Assistance (SEA) provides new and experienced agricultural exporters with the information they need to get their products overseas, on time, in good condition, and at the lowest cost. SEA staff members also conduct export transportation seminars to teach new or prospective agricultural exporters how to transport their high-value or value-added food products overseas. These seminars, which are held throughout the country, cover an array of transportation issues such as finding a freight forwarder, selecting transportation options, packaging, loading containers, and managing temperatures.

Contact: To learn more, call Jim Caron or another SEA staff member at (202) 690-1304, fax (202) 690-3616, or e-mail *jim.caron@usda.gov*. SEA's home page is *www.ams.usda.gov/tmd/tmdsea.htm*.

Transportation Publications and Resources, U.S. Department of

Transportation Publications and Resources are available to help agricultural exporters efficiently use transportation resources and maintain product quality in transit. A weekly grain transportation newsletter, a monthly ocean container rate bulletin, a 10-year database of ocean freight costs for international grain shipments, and special reports are also available. Additionally, technical handbooks are available detailing recommended temperature settings; proper loading procedures for air, truck, and ocean transport; and temperature protection methods.

Contact: To order publications, call the TSB staff at (202) 690-1304, fax (202) 690-3616, or visit *www.ams.usda.gov/tmd/tsb*.

AGRICULTURAL FINANCE AND GRANT PROGRAMS

Export Credit Guarantee Programs, U.S. Department of Agriculture

The Commodity Credit Corporation (CCC) administers a variety of export credit guarantee programs for commercial financing of U.S. agricultural exports. The programs encourage exports to buyers in countries where credit is necessary to maintain or increase U.S. sales but where financing may not be available without CCC guarantees. Because payment is guaranteed, financial institutions in the United States can offer competitive credit terms to the foreign banks, usually with interest rates based on the London inter-bank offered rate (LIBOR). Program announcements issued by USDA provide information on specific country and commodity allocations, length of credit period, and other program information and requirements. Some specific programs are described below:

- The Export Credit Guarantee Program (GSM-102) underwrites credit extended by the private banking sector in the United States (or, less commonly, by a U.S. exporter) to approved foreign banks using dollar-denominated, irrevocable letters of credit to pay for food and agricultural products sold to foreign buyers. GSM-102 covers credit terms up to three years. Under GSM-102, the CCC does not provide financing but guarantees payments due from foreign banks.

- The Supplier Credit Guarantee Program (SCGP) provides a guarantee, in the event of an importer's default, on a portion of a U.S. exporter's open account receivable on terms up to 180 days. U.S. exporters can purchase coverage for agricultural commodities or product sales if short-term credit has been extended directly to the importer. The payment obligation of the importer must be secured by a promissory note signed by the importer as prescribed by the CCC. Although the SCGP emphasizes high-value or value-added agricultural commodities, any agricultural product may be considered.
- The Facility Guarantee Program (FGP) provides credit guarantees for the sale of manufactured goods and services to enhance and establish agribusiness-related facilities overseas that primarily handle, store, distribute, or process U.S. agricultural products and commodities. The FGP assists importers in acquiring needed manufactured goods and services while protecting exporters from most of the risk of non-payment by foreign banks.

Contact: To learn more about any of these programs, call Export Credits at (202) 720-6301, fax (202) 690-0727, e-mail *AskEC@fas.usda.gov*, or visit *www.fas.usda.gov/excredits*.

Market Access Program, Foreign Agricultural Service, U.S. Department of Agriculture

The Market Access Program (MAP) uses funds from the USDA's Commodity Credit Corporation to help U.S. producers, exporters, private companies, and other trade organizations finance both brand and generic promotional activities for U.S. agricultural, fish, and forestry products. The MAP encourages the development, maintenance, and expansion of commercial export markets for these products. Activities financed include consumer promotions, market research, technical assistance, and trade servicing. Agricultural trade organizations, cooperatives, state departments of agriculture, and small businesses may submit applications for participation. The deadline date is published annually in the *Federal Register*.

Contact: For more information, call the Marketing Operations staff at (202) 720-4327, fax (202) 720-9361, or visit *www.fas.usda.gov/mos/programs/mapprog.html*.

CHAPTER 9

HEALTH, PERFORMANCE, QUALITY, AND SAFETY INSPECTION/CERTIFICATION PROGRAMS

U.S.–European Union Safe Harbor Privacy Program, ITA, U.S. Department of Commerce

The Safe Harbor is a voluntary, self-certification system designed to help U.S. companies avoid interruptions in their business dealings with the European Union (EU) or prosecution by European authorities under European privacy laws. The EU Directive on Data Protection took effect in 1998 and prohibits the transfer of personally identifiable information to non-EU nations that fail to meet the European "adequacy" standard for privacy protection. As a result of the differing approaches to privacy established by the European Commission and the United States, this EU directive could significantly hamper the ability of U.S. companies to engage in many trans-Atlantic transactions, including e-commerce. The Safe Harbor framework was developed by the Department of Commerce, in consultation with the EU, industry, and non-governmental organizations, to bridge these different privacy approaches and provide a streamlined means for U.S. organizations to comply with the EU directive.

Contact: Certification may be submitted via the Internet or by sending a letter to Shannon Ballard and Lauren Saadat, Room 2003, International Trade Administration, Department of Commerce, 14th and Constitution Avenue, NW, Washington, DC 20230; (202) 482-3709; fax (202) 482-5522, or e-mail *Shannon.Ballard@mail.doc.gov*, or *Lauren.Saadat@mail.doc.gov*. The home page is *www.export.gov/safeharbor*.

Food and Drug Administration, FDA Export Certificates for U.S. Products

Foreign customers and governments often request that U.S. companies submit an export certificate when they ship products regulated by the Food and Drug Administration (FDA) abroad. FDA export certificates are for export purposes only and may not be used in domestic advertising or promotion. The FDA, at the request of U.S. exporters, will issue export certificates for human drugs and biological products, animal drugs, and medical devices that meet the applicable requirements of the Federal Food, Drug, and Cosmetic Act. The FDA certifies that the products meet domestic U.S. requirements and are eligible for sale in the United States or, in cases where the product may not be marketed in the United States, that the product may be exported under U.S. law. The type of application and information required may differ according to the type of certificate requested and the commodity being exported. Exporters are urged to contact the appropriate center within the FDA for guidance on requesting procedures and export certificate eligibility for their particular country.

Contact: A general information document, *Guidance for Industry—FDA Export Certificates*, is available at *www.fda.gov/cber/gdlns/exprtcert.htm*. The FDA home page, *www.fda.gov*, also provides links to FDA centers. For certificates relating to drugs, contact the Center for Drug Evaluation and Research at (301) 827-8983; for biologics, contact the Center for Biologics Evaluation and Research at (301) 827-6201; for medical devices, contact the Center for Devices and Radiological Health, Office of Compliance, Information Processing, and Office of Automation Branch, at (301) 827-4555, ext. 110; and for animal drugs, contact the Center for Veterinary Medicine at (301) 827-0178.

Inspection Certificates for Food and Agricultural Exports, U.S. Department of Agriculture

Several agencies within the USDA provide inspection services when certificates are required to clear imported products through overseas customs or when requested by foreign buyers:

- The Animal and Plant Health Inspection Service (APHIS) provides exporters information on import and export requirements for plant and animal products and by-products. Phytosanitary inspections for plant materials are offered at ports and interior locations. Animal health certificates for animal products, including hides and pet foods, can be obtained from your local APHIS veterinarian.

Contact: For plant export certification, call (301) 734-8537; for animal health certification, call (301) 734-3277. Visit the APHIS home page at *www.aphis.usda.gov*, and look for "Plant/ Animal/Health."

- The Federal Grain Inspection Service (FGIS) provides inspections under the U.S. Grain Standards Act and the Agricultural Marketing Act. The FGIS also conducts mandatory inspections for all exported grain. Products examined by the FGIS include rice, peas, beans, lentils, all grains, and grain-based processed products.

Contact: For more information, call Robert Lijewski, Standards and Procedures Branch, (202) 720-0252, fax (202) 720-1015, e-mail *robert.s.lijewski@usda.gov*, or visit *www.usda.gov/gipsa*.

- The Food Safety and Inspection Service (FSIS) guarantees that meat and poultry products are properly labeled and U.S. inspected and approved.

Contact: Call the FSIS at (402) 221-7400; fax (402) 221-7479, or visit *www.fsis.usda.gov*.

- The USDA's Agricultural Marketing Service (AMS), in cooperation with state agencies, offers official grading, inspection, and certification services; production and processing verification services; and chemical and microbiological testing services for a variety of agricultural products, including organic products. Grading, inspection, and certification services can be based on U.S. grade standards developed by the USDA for these products, or they can be based on applicant specifications and processes.

Contact: For more information about this voluntary food quality certification service, call Kenneth C. Clayton, associate administrator, AMS, at (202) 720-4276, fax (202) 720-8477, or e-mail *kenneth.clayton@usda.gov*. The home page is *www.ams.usda.gov/index.htm*. AMS program areas include cotton—*www.ams.usda.gov/cotton*, dairy—*www.ams.usda.gov/dairy*, fruits and vegetables—*www.ams.usda.gov/fv*, livestock and seed—*www.ams.usda.gov/lsg*, poultry—*www.ams.usda.gov/poultry*, science and technology—*www.ams.usda.gov/science, tobacco—www.ams.usda.gov/tob*, and transportation and marketing—*www.ams.usda.gov/tmd*, and *www.ams.usda.gov/civilrights*. The AMS International Services home page is *www.ams.usda.gov/international*.

Seafood Inspection Program, National Oceanic and Atmospheric Administration, U.S. Department of Commerce

The National Oceanic and Atmospheric Administration (NOAA) Seafood Inspection Program includes consumer safety officers and trade specialists who offer a range of services to assist U.S. fishing industry businesses engaged in the exports of fish and fishery products. Besides inspecting and certifying products for export, staff members advise seafood marketers about foreign regulations and maintain contact with foreign government regulatory agencies to resolve sanitary and hygienic issues. NOAA also promotes and facilitates the trade of U.S. fishery products internationally. The Seafood Inspection Program can verify, through on-site audits, that foreign processors meet U.S. Food and Drug Administration and U.S. Department of Commerce regulations governing the control of food safety hazards and sanitary hygienic conditions including the construction and maintenance of facilities and equipment, processing techniques, and employee practices in the production of fishery products for human consumption.

Contact: For more information, call Kimberly Young, Seafood Inspection Program, (800) 422-2750 or (301) 713-2355; fax (301) 713-1081; or visit *http://seafood.nmfs.noaa.gov*.

Environmental Technology Verification Program, U.S. Environmental Protection Agency

The Environmental Technology Verification (ETV) program verifies the performance characteristics of commercial-ready environmental technologies through the evaluation of objective, quality-assured data. The program provides potential purchasers and permitters, in the United States and abroad, with an independent and credible assessment of innovative environmental technologies. This voluntary program currently verifies technologies in the following categories: drinking water systems, site characterization and monitoring, innovative coatings and coating equipment, indoor air products, advanced monitoring systems, air pollution control technology, greenhouse gas technology, wet weather flow technologies, and source water protection technologies. A center for verifying pollution prevention, recycling, and waste treatment technologies is being planned.

Contact: To learn more, visit the ETV home page at *www.epa.gov/etv*.

Wholesaler's Basic Permit, Alcohol and Tobacco Tax and Trade Bureau, U.S. Department of the Treasury

A Wholesaler's Basic Permit from the Tobacco Tax and Trade Bureau (TTB), the agency that administers regulations relating to alcohol beverages, is required to export wine, beer, and distilled spirits on a wholesale level. A background check is required before issuance of a Wholesaler's Basic Permit. The United States does not require a permit for alcohol sold abroad on a retail level. The foreign country may mandate specific documentation. Specialists at TTB can help companies navigate the application process.

Contact: To find out how to apply for a permit, call the National Revenue Center at (877) 882-3277 (toll free) or (513) 684-3334, or visit *www.ttb.gov*.

CHAPTER 10

EXPORT LICENSES AND CONTROLS

Bureau of Industry and Security, U.S. Department of Commerce

The Bureau of Industry and Security (BIS) provides assistance on export licensing requirements through its Office of Exporter Services (OEXS). OEXS interprets the Export Administration Regulations (EAR) and provides detailed and up-to-date information on the status of pending license applications. OEXS also offers guidance on a broad range of export issues, including licensing requirements, license-processing time frames, documentation required for export transactions, and country-specific policies. In addition, OEXS counselors can serve as intermediaries and arrange meetings between exporters and BIS licensing officials. OEXS also authorizes emergency processing on export license applications for cases that meet specific and limited criteria.

BIS's Internet-based Simplified Network Application Process (SNAP) provides a secure environment for the electronic submission of license applications, commodity classification requests, and high-performance computer notices. Once OEXS has received and processed a request to use SNAP, exporters can access the system for tracking purposes within 24 hours, and notification of final action is sent electronically.

Contact: For more information, call the BIS Office of Outreach and Educational Services at (202) 482-4811 or fax (202) 482-3617. To speak to an export seminar staff member, call (202) 482-6031 or fax (202) 482-3322. Call the BIS Western Regional Office at (949) 660-0144 or fax (949) 660-9347. Call the BIS Northern California Office at (408) 998-7402 or fax (408) 998-7470. The home page for BIS is *www.bis.doc.gov*.

Office of Foreign Assets Control, U.S. Department of the Treasury

The Office of Foreign Assets Control (OFAC) administers and enforces economic and trade sanctions against targeted foreign countries, terrorists, and international narcotics traffickers and their agents in accordance with U.S. foreign policy and national security goals. OFAC publishes an extensive library of free materials on its Web site to help the international trade community comply with U.S. sanctions. The web site includes summaries of sanctions programs by country, as well as a booklet titled *Foreign Assets Control Regulations for Exporters and Importers*. Also available is the "Specially Designated Nationals and Blocked Persons" list of entities and individuals with whom U.S. persons may not conduct business and whose property must be blocked if under the control of a U.S. person. Users can keep current with OFAC updates through a free subscription e-mail service. All of the information available on the Web site is also available through OFAC's free fax-on-demand service. OFAC also maintains a hotline staffed by compliance officers who are knowledgeable about international trade. They are available Monday through Friday (7:00 a.m. to 7:00 p.m. EST) to provide guidance on sanctions-related matters. The public also has the opportunity to provide comments or ask questions via OFAC's Web site.

Contact: To learn more, call the telephone hotline at (800) 540-6322 or fax (202) 622-2426. The 24-hour fax-on-demand number is (202) 622-0077. The home page is *www.treas.gov/ofac*.

Directorate of Defense Trade Controls, U.S. Department of State

The Directorate of Defense Trade Controls administers section 38 of the Arms Export Control Act and its implementing regulations, the International Traffic in Arms Regulations, in regulating the export and brokering of U.S. defense articles, services, and related technical data covered by the U.S. Munitions List. The directorate, comprised of four offices (Licensing, Compliance, Management, and Policy), adjudicates arms export license applications and ensures export compliance in furtherance of U.S. national security and foreign policy objectives.

Contact: For more information, call the directorate at (202) 663-1281 or (202) 663-2980, or visit *www.pmdtc.org*.

APPENDIX A

EXPORT ASSISTANCE CENTER NETWORK

ALABAMA

Birmingham

950 22nd Street North, Room 707
Birmingham, AL 35203
Phone: (205) 731-1331
Fax: (205) 731-0076
E-mail: *office.birmingham@mail.doc.gov*

ALASKA

Anchorage

31 West 7th Avenue, Suite 108
Anchorage, AK 99501
Phone: (907) 271-6237
Fax: (907) 271-6242
E-mail: *alaska.office.box@mail.doc.gov*

ARIZONA

Phoenix

2901 North Central Avenue, Suite 970
Phoenix, AZ 85012
Phone: (602) 640-2513
Fax: (602) 640-2518
E-mail: *phoenix.office.box@mail.doc.gov*

Tucson

255 West Alameda, 3rd Floor
Tucson, AZ 85701
Phone: (520) 670-5540
Fax: (520) 791-5413
E-mail: *tucson.office.box@mail.doc.gov*

ARKANSAS

Little Rock

425 West Capitol Avenue, Suite 700
Little Rock, AR 72201
Phone: (501) 324-5794
Fax: (501) 324-7380
E-mail: *office.littlerock@mail.doc.gov*

CALIFORNIA

Bakersfield (Kern County)

2100 Chester Avenue, 1st Floor, Suite 166
Bakersfield, CA 93301
Phone: (661) 637-0136
Fax: (661) 637-0156
E-mail: *bakersfield.office.box@mail.doc.gov*

Fresno

550 East Shaw Avenue, Suite 155
Fresno, CA 93710
Phone: (559) 227-6582
Fax: (559) 227-6509
E-mail: *fresno.office.box@mail.doc.gov*

Indio/Cabazon

84-245 Indio Springs Parkway
Indio, CA 92203-3499
Phone: (760) 342-4455
Fax: (760) 342-3535
E-mail: *cynthia.torres@mail.doc.gov*

Inland Empire
2940 Inland Empire Boulevard, Suite 121
Ontario, CA 91764
Phone: (909) 466-4134
Fax: (909) 466-4140
E-mail: *ontario.office.box@mail.doc.gov*

Los Angeles (Downtown)
444 South Flower Street, 34th Floor
Los Angeles, CA 90071
Phone: (213) 894-4231
Fax: (213) 894-8789
E-mail: *los.angeles.downtown.office.box@mail.doc.gov*

Los Angeles (West)
11150 Olympic Boulevard, Suite 975
Los Angeles, CA 90064
Phone: (310) 235-7104
Fax: (310) 235-7220
E-mail: *los.angeles.office.box@mail.doc.gov*

Monterey
411 Pacific Street, Suite 316A
Monterey, CA 93940
Phone: (831) 641-9850
Fax: (831) 641-9849
E-mail: *montereyca.office.box@mail.doc.gov*

Newport Beach
3300 Irvine Avenue, Suite 305
Newport Beach, CA 92660
Phone: (949) 660-1688
Fax: (949) 660-1338
E-mail: *newport.beach.office.box@mail.doc.gov*

Oakland
1301 Clay Street, Suite 630N
Oakland, CA 94612
Phone: (510) 273-7350
Fax: (510) 273-7352
E-mail: *oakland.office.box@mail.doc.gov*

Sacramento
917 7th Street, 2nd Floor
Sacramento, CA 95814
Phone: (916) 498-5155
Fax: (916) 498-5923
E-mail: *sacramento.office.box@mail.doc.gov*

San Diego
6363 Greenwich Drive, Suite 230
San Diego, CA 92122
Phone: (619) 557-5395
Fax: (619) 557-6176
E-mail: *san.diego.office.box@mail.doc.gov*

San Francisco
250 Montgomery Street, 14th Floor
San Francisco, CA 94104
Phone: (415) 705-2300
Fax: (415) 705-2297
E-mail: *san.francisco.office.box@mail.doc.gov*

San Jose
152 North 3rd Street, Suite 550
San Jose, CA 95112-5591
Phone: (408) 271-7300
Fax: (408) 271-7306
E-mail: *san.joseca.office.box@mail.doc.gov*

San Rafael (North Bay/Novato)
4040 Civic Center Drive, Suite 200
San Rafael, CA 94903
Phone: (415) 492-4546/4548
Fax: (415) 492-4549
E-mail: *novato.office.box@mail.doc.gov*

Ventura County
333 Ponoma Street
Port Hueneme, CA 93041
Phone: (805) 488-4844
Fax: (805) 488-7801
E-mail: *gerald.vaughn@mail.doc.gov*

COLORADO

Denver
World Trade Center
1625 Broadway, Suite 680
Denver, CO 80202
Phone: (303) 844-6001
Fax: (303) 844-5651
E-mail: *denver.office.box@mail.doc.gov*

CONNECTICUT

Middletown
213 Court Street, Suite 903
Middletown, CT 06457-3382
Phone: (860) 638-6950
Fax: (860) 638-6970
E-mail: *office.middletown@mail.doc.gov*

DELAWARE

Served by the Philadelphia, Pennsylvania, Export Assistance Center

DISTRICT OF COLUMBIA

Served by the Arlington, Virginia (Northern Virginia), Export Assistance Center

FLORIDA

Clearwater
13805 58th Street North, Suite 1-200
Clearwater, FL 33760
Phone: (727) 893-3738
Fax: (727) 893-3839
E-mail: *office.clearwater@mail.doc.gov*

Ft. Lauderdale
200 East Las Olas Boulevard, Suite 1600
Ft. Lauderdale, FL 33301
Phone: (954) 356-6640
Fax: (954) 356-6644
E-mail: *office.miami@mail.doc.gov*

Jacksonville
3 Independent Drive
Jacksonville, FL 32202
Phone: (904) 232-1270
Fax: (904) 232-1271
E-mail: *office.jacksonville@mail.doc.gov*

Miami
5835 Blue Lagoon Drive, Suite 203
Miami, FL 33126
Phone: (305) 526-7425, ext. 22
Fax: (305) 526-7434
E-mail: *office.miami@mail.doc.gov*

Orlando
200 East Robinson Street, Suite 1270
Orlando, FL 32801
Phone: (407) 648-6235
Fax: (407) 648-6756
E-mail: *office.orlando@mail.doc.gov*

Tallahassee
The Atrium Building
325 John Knox Road, Suite 201
Tallahassee, FL 32303
Phone: (850) 942-9635
Fax: (850) 922-9595
E-mail: *office.tallahassee@mail.doc.gov*

GEORGIA

Atlanta
Centergy One Building
75 Fifth Street, NW, Suite 1055
Atlanta, GA 30308
Phone: (404) 897-6090
Fax: (404) 897-6085
E-mail: *office.atlanta@mail.doc.gov*

Savannah
111 East Liberty Street, Suite 202
Savannah, GA 31405
Phone: (912) 652-4204
Fax: (912) 652-4241
E-mail: *office.savannah@mail.doc.gov*

HAWAII AND THE PACIFIC ISLANDS

Honolulu
521 Ala Moana Boulevard, Room 214
Honolulu, HI 96813
Phone: (808) 522-8040
Fax: (808) 522-8045
E-mail: *honolulu.office.box@mail.doc.gov*

IDAHO

Boise
700 West State Street, 2nd Floor
Boise, ID 83720
Phone: (208) 334-7791
Fax: (208) 334-2783
E-mail: *boise.office.box@mail.doc.gov*

ILLINOIS

Chicago
200 West Adams Street, Suite 2450
Chicago, IL 60606
Phone: (312) 353-8040
Fax: (312) 353-8120
E-mail: *office.chicago@mail.doc.gov*

Libertyville
28055 Ashley Circle, Suite 212
Libertyville, IL 60048
Phone: (847) 327-9082
Fax: (847) 247-0423
E-mail: *office.libertyville@mail.doc.gov*

Peoria
922 North Glenwood Avenue
Jobst Hall, Room 141
Peoria, IL 61606
Phone: (309) 671-7815
Fax: (309) 671-7818
E-mail: *peoria.office.box@mail.doc.gov*

Rockford
515 North Court Street
Rockford, IL 61103
Phone: (815) 987-8123
Fax: (815) 963-7943
E-mail: *office.rockford@mail.doc.gov*

INDIANA

Indianapolis
11405 North Pennsylvania Street, Suite 106
Carmel, IN 46032
Phone: (317) 582-2300
Fax: (317) 582-2301
E-mail: *office.indianapolis@mail.doc.gov*

IOWA

Des Moines
Partnership Building
700 Locust Street, Suite 100
Des Moines, IA 50309
Phone: (515) 288-8614
Fax: (515) 288-1437
E-mail: *des.moines.box@mail.doc.gov*

KANSAS

Wichita
209 East William, Suite 300
Wichita, KS 67202-4012
Phone: (316) 263-4067
Fax: (316) 263-8306
E-mail: *office.wichita@mail.doc.gov*

KENTUCKY

Lexington
4th Floor, Lexington Central Library
140 East Main Street
Lexington, KY 40507
Phone: (859) 225-7001
Fax: (859) 225-6501
E-mail: *sara.moreno@mail.doc.gov*

Louisville
601 West Broadway, Room 634B
Louisville, KY 40202
Phone: (502) 582-5066
Fax: (502) 582-6573
E-mail: *office.louisville@mail.doc.gov*

Somerset
P.O. Box 1660
Somerset, KY 42501
Phone: (606) 677-6160
Fax: (606) 677-6161
E-mail: *office.somerset@mail.doc.gov*

LOUISIANA

New Orleans
2 Canal Street, Suite 2710
New Orleans, LA 70130
Phone: (504) 589-6546
Fax: (504) 589-2337
E-mail: *office.neworleans@mail.doc.gov*

Shreveport
Business Education Building, 119H
One University Place
Shreveport, LA 71115-2399
Phone: (318) 676-3064
Fax: (318) 676-3063
E-mail: *office.shreveport@mail.doc.gov*

MAINE

Portland
c/o Maine International Trade Center
511 Congress Street
Portland, ME 04101
Phone: (207) 541-7400
Fax: (207) 541-7420
E-mail: *info@mitc.org*

MARYLAND

Baltimore
World Trade Center
401 East Pratt Street, Suite 2432
Baltimore, MD 21202
Phone: (410) 962-4539
Fax: (410) 962-4529
E-mail: *obaltimo@mail.doc.gov*

MASSACHUSETTS

Boston
World Trade Center
164 Northern Avenue, Suite 307
Boston, MA 02210
Phone: (617) 424-5990
Fax: (617) 424-5992
E-mail: *office.boston@mail.doc.gov*

MICHIGAN

Detroit
211 West Fort Street, Suite 1104
Detroit, MI 48226
Phone: (313) 226-3650
Fax: (313) 226-3657
E-mail: *office.detroit@mail.doc.gov*

Grand Rapids

401 West Fulton Street, Suite 349-C
Grand Rapids, MI 49504
Phone: (616) 458-3564
Fax: (616) 458-3872
E-mail: *office.grandrapids@mail.doc.gov*

Pontiac

250 Elizabeth Lake Road, Suite 1300 West
Pontiac, MI 48341
Phone: (248) 975-9600
Fax: (248) 975-9606
E-mail: *office.pontiac@mail.doc.gov*

Ypsilanti

c/o Eastern Michigan University
300 West Michigan Avenue
Room 306G, Owen
Ypsilanti, MI 48197
Phone: (734) 487-0259
Fax: (734) 485-2396

MINNESOTA

Minneapolis

45 South 7th Street, Plaza VII, Suite 2240
Minneapolis, MN 55402
Phone: (612) 348-1638
Fax: (612) 348-1650
E-mail: *office.minneapolis@mail.doc.gov*

MISSISSIPPI

Jackson

175 East Capitol Street, Suite 255
Jackson, MS 39201
Phone: (601) 965-4130
Fax: (601) 965-4132
E-mail: *william.scaggs@mail.doc.gov*

MISSOURI

Kansas City

2345 Grand Boulevard, Suite 650
Kansas City, MO 64108
Phone: (816) 426-6285
Fax: (816) 426-6292
E-mail: *office.kansascity@mail.doc.gov*

St. Louis

8235 Forsyth Boulevard, Suite 520
St. Louis, MO 63105
Phone: (314) 425-3302
Fax: (314) 425-3381
E-mail: *office.stlouis@mail.doc.gov*

MONTANA

Missoula

P.O. Box 7487
Missoula, MT 59807
Phone: (406) 542-6656
Fax: (406) 542-6659
E-mail: *montana.office.box@mail.doc.gov*

NEBRASKA

Omaha

11135 O Street
Omaha, NE 68137
Phone: (402) 597-0193
Fax: (402) 597-0194
E-mail: *omaha.office.box@mail.doc.gov*

NEVADA

Las Vegas

400 Las Vegas Boulevard South
Las Vegas, NV 89101
Phone: (702) 366-9406
Fax: (702) 366-0688

Reno
1 East 1st Street, 16th Floor
Reno, NV 89501
Phone: (775) 784-5203
Fax: (775) 784-5343
E-mail: *reno.office.box@mail.doc.gov*

NEW HAMPSHIRE

Portsmouth
17 New Hampshire Avenue
Portsmouth, NH 03801-2838
Phone: (603) 334-6074
Fax: (603) 334-6110
E-mail: *office.portsmouth@mail.doc.gov*

NEW JERSEY

Newark
744 Broad Street, Suite 1505
Newark, NJ 07102
Phone: (973) 645-4682
Fax: (973) 645-4783
E-mail: *office.newark@mail.doc.gov*

Trenton
20 West State Street
P.O. Box 820
Trenton, NJ 08625-0820
Phone: (609) 989-2100
Fax: (609) 989-2395
E-mail: *office.trenton@mail.doc.gov*

NEW MEXICO

Santa Fe
c/o New Mexico Department of
Economic Development
1100 Saint Francis Drive
Sante Fe, NM 87505
Phone: (505) 827-0350
Fax: (505) 827-0263
E-mail: *santa.fe.office.box@mail.doc.gov*

NEW YORK

Buffalo
111 West Huron Street, Room 1304
Buffalo, NY 14202
Phone: (716) 551-4191
Fax: (716) 551-5290
E-mail: *office.buffalo@mail.doc.gov*

Harlem
163 West 125th Street, Suite 901
New York, NY 10027
Phone: (212) 860-6200
Fax: (212) 860-6203
E-mail: *office.harlem@mail.doc.gov*

Long Island
400 County Seat Drive, Suite 046
Mineola, NY 11501
Phone: (516) 739-1765
Fax: (516) 739-3310
E-mail: *office.longisland@mail.doc.gov*

New York City
20 Exchange Plaza, 40th Floor
New York, NY 10005
Phone: (212) 809-2675
Fax: (212) 809-2687
E-mail: *office.newyork@mail.doc.gov*

Rochester
400 Andrews Street, Suite 710
Rochester, NY 14604
Phone: (585) 263-6480
Fax: (585) 325-6505
E-mail: *erin.cole@mail.doc.gov*

Westchester
707 Westchester Avenue, Suite 209
White Plains, NY 10604
Phone: (914) 682-6712
Fax: (914) 682-6698
E-mail: *office.westchester@mail.doc.gov*

NORTH CAROLINA

Charlotte
521 East Morehead Street, Suite 435
Charlotte, NC 28202
Phone: (704) 333-4886
Fax: (704) 332-2681
E-mail: *office.charlottesc@mail.doc.gov*

Greensboro
342 North Elm Street
Greensboro, NC 27401
Phone: (336) 333-5345
Fax: (336) 333-5158
E-mail: *office.greensboro@mail.doc.gov*

Raleigh
Triangle Export Assistance Center
10900 World Trade Boulevard, Suite 110
Raleigh, NC 27617
Phone: (919) 281-2750
Fax: (919) 281-2754
E-mail: *office.raleigh@mail.doc.gov*

NORTH DAKOTA

Served by the Minneapolis, Minnesota, Export Assistance Center

OHIO

Akron
One Cascade Plaza, 17th Floor
Akron, OH 44308
Phone: (330) 237-1264
Fax: (330) 375-5612
E-mail: *office.akron@mail.doc.gov*

Cincinnati
36 East 7th Street, Suite 2650
Cincinnati, OH 45202
Phone: (513) 684-2944
Fax: (513) 684-3227
E-mail: *office.cincinnati@mail.doc.gov*

Cleveland
600 Superior Avenue, East, Suite 700
Cleveland, OH 44114
Phone: (216) 522-4750
Fax: (216) 522-2235
E-mail: *office.cleveland@mail.doc.gov*

Columbus
280 North High Street, Suite 1400
Columbus, OH 43215
Phone: (614) 365-9510
Fax: (614) 365-9598
E-mail: *office.columbus@mail.doc.gov*

Toledo
300 Madison Avenue, Suite 270
Toledo, OH 43604
Phone: (419) 241-0683
Fax: (419) 241-0684
E-mail: *office.toledo@mail.doc.gov*

OKLAHOMA

Oklahoma City
301 Northwest 63rd Street, Suite 330
Oklahoma City, OK 73116
Phone: (405) 608-5302
Fax: (405) 608-4211
E-mail: *oklahomacity.office.box@mail.doc.gov*

Tulsa

700 North Greenwood Avenue, Suite 1400
Tulsa, OK 74106
Phone: (918) 581-7650
Fax: (918) 581-6263
E-mail: *office.tulsa@mail.doc.gov*

OREGON

Portland

One World Trade Center
121 SW Salmon Street, Suite 242
Portland, OR 97204
Phone: (503) 326-3001
Fax: (503) 326-6351
E-mail: *portlandor.office.box@mail.doc.gov*

PENNSYLVANIA

Harrisburg

P.O. Box 11698 (or)
228 Walnut Street, Room 850
Harrisburg, PA 17108-1698
Phone: (717) 221-4510
Fax: (717) 221-4505
E-mail: *office.harrisburg@mail.doc.gov*

Philadelphia

The Curtis Center, Suite 580 West
601 Walnut Street
Philadelphia, PA 19106
Phone: (215) 597-6101
Fax: (215) 597-6123
E-mail: *office.philadelphia@mail.doc.gov*

Pittsburgh

425 6th Avenue, Suite 2950
Pittsburgh, PA 15219
Phone: (412) 644-2800
Fax: (412) 644-2803
E-mail: *office.pittsburgh@mail.doc.gov*

PUERTO RICO

San Juan (Hato Rey)

420 Ponce de Leon Avenue
Midtown Building, 10th Floor
San Juan, PR 00918
Phone: (787) 775-1992
Fax: (787) 766-5692
E-mail: *office.sanjuanpr@mail.doc.gov*

RHODE ISLAND

Providence

One West Exchange Street
Providence, RI 02903
Phone: (401) 528-5104
Fax: (401) 528-5067
E-mail: *office.providence@mail.doc.gov*

SOUTH CAROLINA

Charleston

5300 International Boulevard, Suite 201-C
North Charleston, SC 29418
Phone: (843) 760-3794
Fax: (843) 760-3798
E-mail: *office.charlestonsc@mail.doc.gov*

Columbia

1201 Main Street, Suite 1720
Columbia, SC 29201
Phone: (803) 765-5345
Fax: (803) 253-3614
E-mail: *office.columbia@mail.doc.gov*

Upstate

555 North Pleasantburg Drive
Building 1, Suite 109
Greenville, SC 29607
Phone: (864) 271-1976
Fax: (864) 271-4171
E-mail: *ogreenvi@mail.doc.gov*

SOUTH DAKOTA

Sioux Falls

Augustana College
2001 South Summit Avenue
Madsen Center, Room 122
Sioux Falls, SD 57197
Phone: (605) 330-4264
Fax: (605) 330-4266
E-mail: *office.siouxfalls@mail.doc.gov*

TENNESSEE

Knoxville

Historic City
601 West Summit Hill Drive, Suite 300
Knoxville, TN 37902-2011
Phone: (865) 545-4637
Fax: (865) 545-4435
E-mail: *office.knoxville@mail.doc.gov*

Memphis

Buckman Hall
650 East Parkway South, Suite 328
Memphis, TN 38104
Phone: (901) 323-1543
Fax: (901) 320-9128
E-mail: *office.memphis@mail.doc.gov*

Nashville

211 Commerce Street, 3rd Floor, Suite 100
Nashville, TN 37201
Phone: (615) 259-6060
Fax: (615) 259-6064
E-mail: *office.nashville@mail.doc.gov*

TEXAS

Austin

221 East 11th Street, 4th Floor
Austin, TX 78701
(or)
P.O. Box 12428
Austin, TX 78711
Phone: (512) 916-5939
Fax: (512) 916-5940
E-mail: *office.austin@mail.doc.gov*

Fort Worth

808 Throckmorton Street
Fort Worth, TX 76102
Phone: (817) 392-2673
Fax: (817) 392-2668
E-mail: *office.fortworth@mail.doc.gov*

Houston

15600 John F. Kennedy Boulevard, Suite 530
Houston, TX 77032
Phone: (281) 449-9402
Fax: (281) 449-9437
E-mail: *office.houston@mail.doc.gov*

North Texas

1450 Hughes Road, Suite 220
Grapevine, TX 76051
Phone: (817) 310-3744
Fax: (817) 310-3757
E-mail: *north.texas.office.box@mail.doc.gov*

San Antonio

203 South St. Mary's Street, Suite 360
San Antonio, TX 78205
Phone: (210) 228-9878
Fax: (210) 228-9874
E-mail: *Michaelrosales@mail.doc.gov*

South Texas
6401 South 36th Street, Suite 4
McAllen, TX 78503
Phone: (956) 661-0238
Fax: (956) 661-0239
E-mail: *south.texas.office.box@mail.doc.gov*

West Texas
1400 North FM 1788, Room 1303
Midland, TX 79707
Phone: (423) 552-2490
Fax: (432) 552-3490
E-mail: *west.texas.office.box@mail.doc.gov*

UTAH

Salt Lake City
324 South State Street, Suite 221
Salt Lake City, UT 84111
Phone: (801) 524-5116
Fax: (801) 524-5886
E-mail: *salt.lake.city.office.box@mail.doc.gov*

VERMONT

Montpelier
National Life Building, 6th Floor
Montpelier, VT 05620-0501
Phone: (802) 828-4508
Fax: (802) 828-3258
E-mail: *office.montpelier@mail.doc.gov*

VIRGINIA

Arlington (Northern Virginia)
1401 Wilson Boulevard, Suite 1225
Arlington, VA 22209
Phone: (703) 235-0331
Fax: (703) 524-2649
E-mail: *office.nova@mail.doc.gov*

Richmond
P.O. Box 10026
Richmond, VA 23240-0026
(or)
400 North 8th Street, Suite 412
Richmond, VA 23240
Phone: (804) 771-2246
Fax: (804) 771-2390
E-mail: *office.richmond@mail.doc.gov*

WASHINGTON

Seattle
2601 4th Avenue, Suite 320
Seattle, WA 98121
Phone: (206) 553-5615
Fax: (206) 553-7253
E-mail: *seattle.office.box@mail.doc.gov*

Spokane
Spokane Regional Chamber of Commerce
801 West Riverside Avenue, Suite 400
Spokane, WA 99201
Phone: (509) 353-2625
Fax: (509) 353-2449
E-mail: *spokane.office.box@mail.doc.gov*

Tacoma
950 Pacific Avenue, Suite 410
Tacoma, WA 98402
Phone: (253) 593-6736
Fax: (253) 383-4676
E-mail: *tacoma.office.box@mail.doc.gov*

WEST VIRGINIA

Charleston
405 Capitol Street, Suite 807
Charleston, WV 25301
Phone: (304) 347-5123
Fax: (304) 347-5408
E-mail: *charlestonwv.office.box@mail.doc.gov*

Wheeling

c/o Wheeling Jesuit University/NTTC
316 Washington Avenue
Wheeling, WV 26003
Phone: (304) 243-5493
Fax: (304) 243-5494
E-mail: *office.wheeling@mail.doc.gov*

WISCONSIN

Milwaukee

517 East Wisconsin Avenue, Room 596
Milwaukee, WI 53202
Phone: (414) 297-3473
Fax: (414) 297-3470
E-mail: *office.milwaukee@mail.doc.gov*

WYOMING

Served by the Denver, Colorado, Export Assistance Center

APPENDIX B

TRADE PROMOTION COORDINATING COMMITTEE AGENCIES AND ADDRESSES

U.S. Department of Commerce
1401 Constitution Avenue, NW
Washington, DC 20230
www.commerce.gov

U.S. Department of State
2201 C Street, NW
Washington, DC 20520
www.state.gov

U.S. Department of the Treasury
1500 Pennsylvania Avenue, NW
Washington, DC 20220
www.treasury.gov

U.S. Department of Defense
The Pentagon
Washington, DC 20301
www.defense.gov

U.S. Department of the Interior
1849 C Street, NW
Washington, DC 20240
www.interior.gov

U.S. Department of Agriculture
14th Street and Independence Avenue, SW
Washington, DC 20250
www.usda.gov

U.S. Department of Labor
200 Constitution Avenue, NW
Washington, DC 20210
www.labor.gov

U.S. Department of Transportation
400 7th Street, SW
Washington, DC 20590
www.transportation.gov

U.S. Department of Energy
1000 Independence Avenue, SW
Washington, DC 20585
www.energy.gov

Office of Management and Budget
New Executive Office Building
725 17th Street, NW
Washington, DC 20503
www.omb.gov

Office of the United States Trade Representative
600 17th Street, NW
Washington, DC 20508
www.ustr.gov

Council of Economic Advisers
Eisenhower Executive Office Building, Room 99
The White House
Washington, DC 20502
www.whitehouse.gov/cea

Environmental Protection Agency
Ronald Reagan Building, Room 31237
1300 Pennsylvania Avenue, NW
Washington, DC 20460
www.epa.gov

U.S. Small Business Administration
409 3rd Street, SW
Washington, DC 20416
www.sba.gov

U.S. Agency for International Development
State Department Building
320 21st Street, NW
Washington, DC 20523
www.usaid.gov

Export–Import Bank of the United States
811 Vermont Avenue, NW
Washington, DC 20571
www.exim.gov

Overseas Private Investment Corporation
1100 New York Avenue, NW
Washington, DC 20527
www.opic.gov

U.S. Trade and Development Agency
1000 Wilson Boulevard, Suite 1600
Arlington, VA 22209
www.tda.gov

National Economic Council
The White House
Washington, DC 20502
www.whitehouse.gov/nec

FINDING AIDS

LIST OF PROGRAMS BY AGENCY

EXPORT–IMPORT BANK OF THE UNITED STATES

SMALL BUSINESS ADMINISTRATION

U.S. AGENCY FOR INTERNATIONAL DEVELOPMENT (USAID)

U.S. DEPARTMENT OF AGRICULTURE

U.S. DEPARTMENT OF COMMERCE

U.S. DEPARTMENT OF ENERGY

U.S. ENVIRONMENTAL PROTECTION AGENCY

ALPHABETICAL LIST OF PROGRAMS

ACRONYMS AND ABBREVIATIONS

AMDB	Advocacy and Multilateral Developmental Bank
AMS	Agricultural Marketing Service
APHIS	Animal and Plant Health Inspection Service
BIC	Business Information Center
BIS	Bureau of Industry and Security
BISNIS	Business Information Service for the Newly Independent States
BRD	Business Resource Database
CCC	Commodity Credit Corporation
CCG	Country Commercial Guide
CMR	Customized Market Research
CS	U.S. Commercial Service
DAC	Development Assistance Committee
DEC	District Export Council
EAR	Export Administration Regulations
ELAN	Export Legal Assistance Network
ERS	Economic Research Service
E-TAP	Export Trade Assistance Partnership
ETNA	Environmental Technology Network for Asia and the Americas
ETV	Environmental Technology Verification
EU	European Union
Ex–Im Bank	Export–Import Bank
FAS	Foreign Agricultural Service
FDA	Food and Drug Administration
FGIS	Federal Grain Inspection Service
FGP	Facility Guarantee Program
FLT	Foreign Labor Trends
FSIS	Food Safety and Inspection Service
FSO	foreign service officer
GDI	Global Diversity Initiative
GTN	Global Trade & Technology Network
IBP	International Buyer Program
ICP	International Company Profile
IDB	International Data Base
IPS	International Partner Search
ITA	International Trade Administration
MAC	Market Access Compliance
MAP	Market Access Program

MAS	Manufacturing and Services
MBDA	Minority Business Development Agency
MBDC	Minority Business Development Center
MBE	minority business enterprise
MDB	Multilateral Development Bank
NABDC	Native American Business Development Center
NAFTA	North American Free Trade Agreement
NAL	National Agricultural Library
NCSCI	National Center for Standards and Certification Information
NOAA	National Oceanic and Atmospheric Administration
NTIS	National Technical Information Service
OEXS	Office of Exporter Services
OFAC	Office of Foreign Assets Control
OIT	Office of International Trade
OSDBU	Office of Small and Disadvantaged Business Utilization
OTEXA	Small Office of Textiles and Apparel
OTII	Office of Trade and Industry Information
OECD	Organization for Economic Cooperation and Development
OPIC	Overseas Private Investment Corporation
OSAC	Overseas Security Advisory Council
SABIT	Special American Business Internship Training
SBA	Small Business Administration
SBDC	Small Business Development Centers
SBIC	small business investment company
SCGP	Supplier Credit Guarantee Program
SCORE	Service Corps of Retired Executives
SEA	Office of Shipper and Exporter Assistance
SNAP	Simplified Network Application Process
TCC	Trade Compliance Center
TIC	Trade Information Center
TSB	Transportation Services Branch
TTB	Tobacco Tax and Trade Bureau
US-AEP	United States–Asia Environmental Partnership
USAID	U.S. Agency for International Development
USDA	U.S. Department of Agriculture
USEAC	U.S. Export Assistance Center
USTDA	U.S. Trade and Development Agency
USTR	Office of the U.S. Trade Representative

NOTES